The Theory and Practice
of Archaeology

The Theory and Practice of Archaeology

A Workbook

SECOND EDITION

Thomas C. Patterson
Temple University

 PRENTICE HALL, Englewood Cliffs, New Jersey 07632

Editorial/production supervision,
   interior design, and electronic page makeup: Kari Callaghan Mazzola
Acquisitions editor: Nancy Roberts
Cover design: Terrapin Graphics
Cover photo: George Daniell/Photo Researchers
Prepress buyer: Kelly Behr
Manufacturing buyer: Mary Ann Gloriande

© 1994, 1983 by Prentice-Hall, Inc.
A Paramount Communications Company
Englewood Cliffs, New Jersey 07632

Printed in the United States of America
10   9   8   7   6   5   4   3   2   1

ISBN 0-13-014846-6

PRENTICE-HALL INTERNATIONAL (UK) LIMITED, *London*
PRENTICE HALL OF AUSTRALIA PTY. LIMITED, *Sydney*
PRENTICE-HALL CANADA INC., *Toronto*
PRENTICE-HALL HISPANOAMERICANA, S.A., *Mexico*
PRENTICE-HALL OF INDIA PRIVATE LIMITED, *New Delhi*
PRENTICE-HALL OF JAPAN, INC., *Tokyo*
SIMON & SCHUSTER ASIA PTE. LTD., *Singapore*
EDITORA PRENTICE-HALL DO BRASIL, LTDA., *Rio de Janeiro*

Contents

Problem 12

Class Struggle and Resistance   *129*

Preface

This is a workbook. It is the product of more than twenty years of interaction with friends and students, during which I tried to communicate to them how archaeologists learn to think like archaeologists. It is also the product of a belief that the most effective way of learning something is by actually doing it successfully and then using the knowledge gained in the process to solve new problems. This happens in archaeology as it does in carpentry or plumbing or learning to swim.

Archaeology is more than digging holes in the ground to find things. It is also more than building grand theories to explain the origins of food production, the rise and fall of a particular civilization, or the origins and development of a particular human society. Something else occurs in between the excavation—the manual labor, the romance, and the pleasures of field archaeology—and the explanation—the mental activity involved in explaining what excavated materials mean and how they affect our understanding of the ancient society whose men and women produced those remains. The activities that occur in between excavation and explanation take up most of the archaeologist's time and provide the linkage that relates archaeological theory to archaeological practice. This workbook is concerned with those activities. Thus, it is also an attempt to de-mystify what archaeologists actually do.

This workbook consists of twelve problems. Each problem is divided into three parts: (1) a brief introduction to the topic and a description of techniques used to answer certain questions; (2) a presentation of the data and the questions themselves—i.e., The Data and the Problem; and (3) a discussion of how one archaeologist, the author, went about answering the questions—i.e., Discussion of the Problem. Clearly, these are not the only problems of interest to archaeologists, nor are my discussions of them intended to be anything more than inquiries into *one* way of solving these problems.

A good deal of what archaeologists do involves locating sites; describing, sorting, and classifying the evidence they recover from these locations; and, given limited human and financial resources, deciding which of these sites should be studied more thoroughly. I have not focused on surveying, mapping, classification, or sampling strategies in this book. Instead, I have presented information in terms of presumed classificatory schemes—for example, single-warp twined textiles or red-painted pottery—without discussing how these arrangements of evidence were derived. This could be considered a weakness of this work; however, to have delved into the methodological issues of typology, sampling, or the use of quantitative methods would have led to a much longer book, and one with a very different focus.

ACKNOWLEDGMENTS

Many people participated in this project throughout the course of my conceptualizing and writing of both the first edition and this second edition of *The Theory and Practice of Archaeology: A Workbook.* Since 1983, when the first edition appeared, many friends and students have helped me reshape and recast this book. They have provided the intellectual climate and the opportunity for trying out various ideas. I especially want to thank the following persons for their encouragement, help, and constructive criticism: Barbara Bender, Michael Blakey, Sara Bon, Elizabeth Brumfiel, Richard Burger, Carole Crumley, Terrence Epperson, Christine Gailey, Russell Handsman, Patricia Hansell, Susan Kus, Richard Lee, Mark Leone, William Marquardt, Randall McGuire, Rene Millon, Viana Muller, Robert Paynter, Karen Sacks, Karen Spalding, Maurizio Tosi, Raghu Trichur, and Alison Wylie. I also want to thank the reviewers of this edition, who provided constructive feedback and helpful advice.

Finally, I want to thank those of you—and there are now several hundred of you—who have contacted me since the publication of the first edition. You have validated my efforts by taking the time to talk with me at meetings or by writing letters in which you raised questions, pointed out inconsistencies, or argued for other interpretations based on analyses that proceeded from different premises.

Some Suggestions
for Instructors

Reviewers of the first edition expressed concern about how it could be used as a workbook, since the discussions at the end of the book (which have been moved to the end of each chapter in the second edition) provided answers for the very problems the students were asked to solve. Judging by my own experiences and the comments of teachers who used the first edition, providing those answers has not been detrimental to the students' learning process.

The first-edition reviewers were actually asking how instructors could prevent the students from using the answers in the discussion sections as they worked out solutions to the problems. The answer is that they cannot prevent this, nor should they try to do so, since discussions are intended to de-mystify what archaeologists actually do by showing students how one practitioner went about solving the problems. This approach validates the students' own efforts by providing them with a step-by-step model they can refer to as they work through the questions and the evidence. Like the rest of us, students learn by trial-and-success, which often involves seeing how others have done something, emulating that process, having their efforts validated by critical comparison to the endeavors of others, and then trying to improve on what they have done.

In using some or all of these problems in various courses, I encouraged my students to collaborate with one another as they worked through the questions and evidence of each problem. In practice, this meant that students worked in groups of two, three, or four individuals. A different group presented each problem to the remainder of the class. Their presentations consisted of discussions of the questions, evidence, and solutions. More often than not they also included critical commentaries on my analyses, or at least questions about their validity.

My major contribution to the student presentations was to provide an atmosphere in which the teacher-student relationship—which defines the teacher as the dispenser of knowledge and the student as the recipient—could be broken. To do so meant I had to give up part of the traditional role of the teacher and begin learning from my students. This was exciting and rewarding but difficult at times, because I had to listen carefully and often found it hard to graciously accept criticism, constructive or otherwise. (Some friends have suggested that my listening ability and social skills may be improving slowly with age.) I would suggest that instructors using this workbook try to create a similar classroom atmosphere, breaking away from rigid, traditional teacher-student roles.

The Theory and Practice of Archaeology can be used in three different types of courses. The first is an introductory archaeology course in which the twelve problems are used in conjunction with a text on world archaeology. Varying amounts of time (up to roughly one-third of class time) can be devoted to the problems, dealing with how archaeologists use questions, evidence, and theory to paint pictures of what ancient societies were like and how they changed— topics that can become the subject matter for the remainder of the class time.

The second type of course deals with the fundamentals of archaeological method and theory. Here the problems can be used in conjunction with a text on archaeological method and theory. Roughly one-third of class time can be devoted to the problems; another third can be spent clarifying the theoretical or practical issues raised by the problems or the text; and the remaining time can be used to ask questions and discuss archaeological materials from excavated collections, surface collections, or published sources, which will introduce some of the complexity and texture archaeologists actually deal with in their analyses.

The third type of course deals with the interpretation of archaeological evidence, conducted at an advanced undergraduate and beginning graduate level. In this instance, the problems can be used in conjunction with related outside readings in journals and monographs; the basic readings are listed in the reference section for each problem. Roughly a third of the class time can be devoted to the problems, and the remainder can be spent analyzing outside readings and developing a critique of what archaeologists were doing about such topics as the analysis of class and state formation, the construction of landscapes, and the social construction of gender and ethnic identities. These readings and discussions necessarily will expose the students to other topics—such as liberal and Marxist social thought, various strands of feminist thought, population growth, and development or equilibrium models—whose origins and centers of gravity lie outside archaeology. The influence of these views has seemingly become more transparent in the 1990s as archaeologists have begun to acknowledge their debt to and involvement in wider intellectual currents.

Clearly, the theoretical underpinnings of the problems in this book and the issues they address extend beyond the field of archaeology. They are part of a broader debate in the social sciences concerning the nature of human social relations in different kinds of societies, how and why these relationships articulate with each other and vary in different kinds of societies, how they are transformed by the appearance of exploitation, and how power relations, which are ultimately unstable, are resisted. To the extent that the problems in the book focus attention on these debates and pose questions about the theoretical issues raised, they are not only relevant to the debate but also part of it. From this perspective, *The Theory and Practice of Archaeology* is also relevant in courses or contexts other than the ones I have mentioned; it has been used in introductory cultural anthropology courses and can also be used in survey courses in history, sociology, women's studies, classics, and political economy.

The Theory and Practice
of Archaeology

Introduction

Knowledge begins with practice, and theoretical knowledge is acquired through practice and must then return to practice. (Zedong, 1937/1975)

ARCHAEOLOGICAL PRACTICE

While archaeologists often emphasize different facets of what they do, most agree that a major goal of their business is reconstructing particular ancient societies—that is, bringing them back to life. Archaeology is a historical social science whose objective is to understand varied past forms of society, their transformation up to their union with modern societies, and the relations and processes that were the motors driving these changes. This is accomplished by digging up and studying remains that were left by the ancient peoples under study.

Archaeologists, of course, are not the only individuals who are concerned with what ancient societies were like and how they changed. Historians would make the same claim. Clearly, the goals of the archaeologist and the historian are very similar, if not identical. It is also clear that most archaeologists are not historians and that most historians are not archaeologists. What distinguishes them are not the goals of their inquiries—that is, past societies and how and why they have changed—but rather the kinds of evidence they use and the techniques they have developed to deal with this information.

1

Historians rely on written records to reconstruct the past. They recognize that literacy and written documents have usually been closely linked to the needs of states and ruling classes; consequently, they are beginning to understand more clearly that the views and interests of subordinated groups are simply not recorded in many kinds of documents, and that the voices of these groups are frequently muted or silent altogether. Historians have to determine why an author wrote a particular document. They have to determine whether the author was in a position to observe what happened or whether the report is based merely on hearsay. They have to determine the views and biases of the author and, more precisely, those of the literate social class, order, or estate from which the author came. And finally, they have to determine whether the information in the document is accurate or whether it has been distorted or falsified in some fashion, either accidentally or deliberately. Out of necessity, historians have written extensively about ways of assessing the validity and reliability of evidence they use. They continue to do so because of changes in the kinds of questions they ask and the kinds of written records they come to view as evidence.

Archaeologists are not especially concerned about the accuracy of views that ancient peoples had about themselves or, in some contexts, even of the statements they made. Instead, they are concerned with the remains—the objects and their spatial relationships or associations with one another—that were left by ancient peoples at places where they carried out various activities in the past. Archaeologists deal with evidence that was not deliberately left for posterity, and they use evidence for purposes that were very different from those of the people who produced it, just as historians do with the information they use.

Archaeologists have had to develop methods for determining whether or not their information adequately reflects the total range of activities that were characteristic of a particular society at a given place and time in the past. If the remains are not representative of what happened, they have to determine whether their information was distorted by processes that disturb, modify, or destroy the archaeological sites they are investigating or whether it was biased by the collection procedures or techniques they used; for example, failing to collect certain kinds of evidence or to investigate what happened in certain kinds of localities. Since archaeologists are continually asking new questions of the objects and associations they find at archaeological sites, they are continually developing ways of getting new kinds of information from this evidence and assessing its reliability.

This technical division of labor between archaeologists and historians, based on the kinds of evidence and methods they employ to recuperate the past, has potentially unfortunate side effects. It often prevents practitioners of the two disciplines from talking to each other about their common object of inquiry—that is, how and why different kinds of societies change. Sometimes the silence is promoted by chauvinism, which usually takes the form of the "my data are better than your data" taunts we heard and maybe even used in grammar school. Intolerance, prejudice, and parochialism do not promote the exchange of ideas; they do not allow people to play creatively with new ways of understanding or to construct new understandings of past societies.

In other instances, communication between the two disciplines resembles a mugging in which the perpetrators assault the victims, steal their information, and publish it quickly without really understanding what they have taken, the contexts in which it was used, the assets and liabilities of the purloined objects, and what unexpected or unintended consequences their actions will have. In my experience, the most informative conversations between archaeologist and historian occur when they share a common theoretical framework, when each has a textured appreciation of the kinds of information used by the other, and when each can ask questions of the other that are meaningful, given the advantages and limitations of their evidence and methods. In these instances, a shared theoretical understanding, the importance of certain kinds of questions, and the capacity to phrase these in ways that are relevant or meaningful given the limitations of different kinds of evidence are the bridgehead that allows further discussion, negotiation, and insights.

ARCHAEOLOGICAL EVIDENCE

Archaeologists find the kinds of evidence they use to reconstruct what ancient societies were like, how they came to be that way, and how they changed or were transformed into different kinds of societies at archaeological sites. These are places where people did something that modified the natural setting by leaving things that provide clues about what they did. At some sites there may be traces of only a single activity reflected in the remains; for example, someone dropped and broke a pottery vessel filled with beer. Other sites, such as the buried city of Pompeii near Naples, Italy, contain traces of literally hundreds of thousands of activities. Some sites are quite small in that the activities occurred in an area covering only a few square meters, whereas other sites extend continuously over many square kilometers. The activities undertaken at one site may have been carried out during a period of such short duration—a season, a few years—that it is difficult or impossible to distinguish those carried out first from those carried out later. At another site the activities may have been undertaken intermittently over a long period of time, so that it is possible to distinguish between the earlier and later ones.

Archaeologists use two kinds of evidence, *objects* and *associations*, to reconstruct what happened in the past. The objects—items that were manufactured, modified, or moved by people—range in size and complexity from a stone tool or a rock charred in a fireplace to a pyramid. They provide information not only about the productive forces of a society—the natural objects used by a people, the implements they employed to transform these items into goods that satisfied their needs, and knowledge and skills they possessed that enabled them to do so— but about the artistic achievements of its members.

Associations—the spatial arrangements and relationships of objects with respect to each other to features of the environment in which they occur, especially those indicating that the objects and associations were in use at the same time or during the same period—provide additional information about a society's productive forces and artistic achievements that might not be immediately apparent from an examination of just the objects themselves. They also provide information about the various kinds of social and economic relationships that existed in specific ancient societies.

The archaeological record is quite rich, particularly when we go beyond our perceptions of the separateness and uniqueness of the objects and their associations and begin to arrange them in ways that allow us to reconstruct the social reality that they reflect and that produced them. This involves a qualitative shift from elementary ideas that are based on our sensory perceptions of the objects and their spatial arrangement to abstract ideas that are derived by generalization, not from a direct comparison of a number of perceptible objects and associations, but from reflection on the processes and relationships in which they are involved. The question is: How do we make this shift from perceptual knowledge to rational knowledge or theoretical understanding of the materials?

THEORY AND PRACTICE

As the quotation at the beginning of this introduction indicates, its author—certainly one of the more practical social theorists of the twentieth century—had some thoughts about this question and about the relation between perception and the development of systematic theoretical understanding. Basically, he argues that the way in which we learn to do something is by actually doing it successfully rather than by just thinking or reading about it or about how it is done; that theory is ultimately based upon the experience we have already gained by doing something successfully; and that our practice—the way in which we do this thing—is ultimately enhanced by the understanding, or theoretical perspective, that we have gained in the process. In other words, there is a dialectical relationship between theory and practice. Theory informs practice but is ultimately based in it; practice elaborates and refines theory (Zedong 1975).

Archaeologists have practiced archaeology—practicing it as a specialized undertaking with its own distinctive methods, techniques, and kinds of evidence—for enough time that they have come to share a body of facts, concepts, ideas, points of view, and questions about which they are in significant but not complete agreement. These were formed, worked out, tested, and refined as people practiced archaeology in the past. They are used now because they work. They also provide the foundations for future practice and for future discoveries in the field.

Discoveries are made when people ask and successfully answer questions of the archaeological evidence that provide new insights about the kinds of relations and processes that existed, their characteristics, and their interconnections. The content of the discoveries is always expressed or formulated in terms of concepts and ideas that are part of the intellectual baggage of archaeology that has been acquired through successful practice over the years. In other words, there is a difference between the actual content of a discovery and the theoretical perspective or preconceptions in terms of which it always expressed. Consequently, there is a contradiction between the content of a discovery and the way in which it is interpreted or formulated. We can resolve this contradiction in one of two ways. Either we can use the new information to develop new ways of perceiving and understanding what happened, or we can retain the perspective, incorporating the new information into it and, by doing so, inhibit the development of new points of view and new forms of practice in the long run (Cornforth 1955: 102–104).

Archaeologists rarely disagree about the nature of scientific in their field, the nature of evidence, the ways in which competing theoretical ideas and concepts should be assessed, or even the existence of standards of explanation. This high level of agreement is codified in virtually every introductory text dealing with archaeological method and theory that has been written since the 1930s. When archaeologists do disagree, their disputes over methodology are often vehement and are usually blown out of proportion, distorted, and reported as major theoretical debates in the field. In fact, they are often nothing more than minor skirmishes between individuals who hold slightly variant positions of essentially the same theoretical perspective about the nature of the social realities that underlie the production of all archaeological evidence.

While archaeologists may vigorously debate certain topics—for example, did New World "civilizations" develop independently from those in the Old World?—they have generally refrained from engaging in serious discussion of the very real theoretical disagreements concerning the nature of the social realities underlying the evidence, the implications of these differences, and their significance for future practice. This reflects the uneven development of the social sciences as a whole; the particular place and role of archaeology among them; and the way in which the mental labor involved in developing abstract ideas about what societies are like has been divorced from the elementary ideas we all have about the world we live in—notions that are based on our own perceptions and experience in relating to other people and to the world around us as we try to satisfy our needs.

As a community of practitioners, archaeologists have had a hard time acknowledging the existence of contradictory theoretical perspectives of social reality and an even harder time dealing with the implications that these might have for the future practice of their science. Either they do not recognize or acknowledge the existence of contradictory theoretical viewpoints of social reality, or they try to relegate any discussion of them to some methodological debate. They rewrite the development of the field or of theoretical controversies in it from a particular perspective to make it conform to the tenets of that particular theoretical position; by doing so, they ultimately misrepresent other positions or the conflict itself, because the alternatives are somehow viewed as intellectually, morally, or politically objectionable. They uncritically rehash debates carried out earlier in other fields. Or they mechanically adopt and apply a *theoretical* scaffolding that was erected to account for the scientific development of some distantly related field of scientific inquiry in natural sciences—like theoretical physics.

The specter of relativism challenges a deeply held and cherished belief among many archaeologists. That is, there are universally valid criteria of truth and rationality. However, the existence of multiple standpoints does not necessarily challenge the notion that "there is a real world out there" that exists independently of the cognitive facilities of knowing subjects—like archaeologists. These multiple understandings do imply that there is a systematic relationship between the existential conditions or positions of various groups, whose members include archaeologists, and the content of the knowledge and/or understandings they have of the world.

If we acknowledge the existence of multiple perspectives, then we have to identify the various viewpoints, explain their interrelationships, and justify the rationale for choosing one over another. Of course, this is precisely what happened in the 1980s. Social scientists, including some archaeologists, began to examine the nature of these fundamental theoretical disagreements and their implications for practice (e.g., Benton 1977; Gathercole & Lowenthal 1990; Gero & Conkey 1991; Harding 1986; Hodder 1991; Pateman 1988; Trigger 1989). Inquiries into the foundations of various theoretical positions concerned with the nature of human societies and their development—which neither distort their content nor displace the implications of the disagreement—are critical for the growth of archaeology as a field of scientific inquiry. They are also essential for our understanding of how human society has come to be the way it is today. For archaeology, this will only happen (1) as we begin to appraise and reappraise the evidence provided by the archaeological record through clearly shaped theoretically informed lenses; (2) as we clarify the meaning and implications of different theoretical viewpoints and transform and extend them to explain new situations; and (3) as we assess accurately which standpoints provide us with the greatest understanding of what happened in the past, the most informative line for future inquiry, and the greatest potential for elaborating and refining both our theory and practice. We can accomplish this only through practice itself.

REFERENCES

Benton, Ted. (1977). *Philosophical foundations of the three sociologies.* London & Boston: Routledge & Kegan Paul.

Cornforth, Maurice. (1955). *The theory of knowledge.* New York: International Publishers.

Gathercole, Peter, & David Lowenthal (Eds.). (1990). *The politics of the past.* London: Unwin Hyman.

Gero, Joan M., & Margaret M. Conkey (Eds.). (1991). *Engendering archaeology: Women and prehistory.* Oxford & Cambridge: Basil Blackwell.

Harding, Sandra. (1986). *The science question in feminism.* Ithaca & London: Cornell University Press.

Hodder, Ian. (1991). *Reading the past: Current approaches to interpretation in archaeology.* Cambridge: Cambridge University Press.

Pateman, Carole. (1988). *The sexual contract. Stanford: Stanford University Press.*

Trigger, Bruce G. (1989). *A history of archaeological thought.* Cambridge: Cambridge University Press.

Zedong, Mao. (1975). On practice. In *Selected works of Mao Tse-tung* (Vol. 1, pp. 295–310). Peking: Foreign Language Press. (Original work published 1937.)

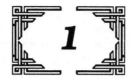

Seriation: Ordering Archaeological Evidence by Stylistic Differences

SERIATION

Seriation involves arranging archaeological materials into a presumed chronological sequence by some technique other than superposition. These materials can range from individual objects of the same kind— such as pottery bowls, tapestry shirts, or chipped stone projectile points—to entire archaeological assemblages—such as grave lots or the objects and associations found in a single stratum. Seriations can be established by a number of different techniques (Cowgill 1972; Marquardt 1978). The major premise underlying all the techniques is that, under most conditions, cultural and stylistic change is a gradual process. Consequently, objects or assemblages that are similar to one another will be closer together in sequence and in age than will ones that are less similar to one another and, therefore, farther apart in time (Rowe 1961). The first seriational argument based on the idea that stylistic change is gradual and that specimens can be dated relative to one another by stylistic differences was made by John Evans in 1849, when he established a sequence for prehistoric British coins (Rouse 1967; Rowe 1961).[1]

1. The idea of dating objects by their style is important in archaeology. It was first proposed by Jean Jacques Barthelemy in 1756 and was put into practice eight years later by Johann Joachim Winckelmann in his *History of Ancient Art*, in which he dated pieces of classical sculpture by relating changes in their style to what ancient writers said about art and to the style of old coins that could be dated (Rowe 1972). The idea of stylistic dating was subsequently expanded to include materials that were prehistoric in the sense that written records, datable coins, or both were not available. By 1836, Christian Jurgensen Thomsen knew enough about the style of bronze objects from Denmark that he could distinguish between those made during the Danish Bronze Age and those made during the Danish Iron Age (Rowe 1962: 129–130).

Seriational arguments are often used in archaeology and have a high degree of credibility when certain conditions are satisfied. First, the objects or assemblages being seriated should belong to the same cultural tradition. Since seriational techniques are based on the assumption that stylistic change is gradual, it is not reasonable to use data from different cultural traditions and regions to establish a single sequence. Second, the materials being seriated should come from a restricted geographical region to eliminate or reduce the possibility of contemporary variation due to social factors or to lags in the spread of features from one part of the area to another (Deetz & Dethlefsen 1965; Dunnell 1970). Third, it is important to recognize situations that can produce sudden changes in the cultural and stylistic traditions of a region: for example, the purely mechanical situation of a break in the local sequence so that the objects or assemblages following the gap in time bear no resemblance to those preceding it, or cultural factors, such as strong outside influences that appear suddenly and swamp the local tradition or a deliberate attempt to revive or imitate earlier features (Cowgill 1972: 384; Rowe 1961: 326–327). Fourth, since no assumption is made about the direction in which change is taking place, it is essential to establish the proper chronological order of the sequence by referring to some kind of external evidence—such as superposition or the presence of datable objects in the seriation. When seriating archaeological materials, be they sets of individual objects or entire assemblages, it is useful to view each object or assemblage as being composed of a number of features. For instance, features of a pottery bottle would be the overall shape of the vessel, the proportion and shape of the neck and spout with respect to the body, the area of the vessel that is decorated, the kind of decoration that is used, and the particular designs that occur.

As an example of one seriational technique, consider three features that might occur on five pottery bottles from the same local area: the height of the neck, the location of the painted design on the vessel, and the colors used to paint the design. Vessel 1 has a tall neck and red-painted decoration on the neck. Vessel 2 has a tall neck and red-painted decoration on the body. Vessel 3 has a short neck and green-painted decoration on the body. Vessel 4 has a tall neck and red-and-blue-painted decoration on the body. Vessel 5 has a short neck and blue-and-green-painted decoration on the body. A convenient way in which to seriate objects is to arrange them in such a way that each feature being examined has a continuous distribution and an overlapping distribution with other features. For example, Vessels 1, 2, and 4 have tall necks, whereas 3 and 5 have short ones. Vessel 1 is the only one with a decorated neck, and Vessel 1 and Vessel 2 are the only ones with exclusively red-painted decoration. Vessels 2 through 5 have decorated bodies and plain necks. Vessels 2 and 4 are the only ones with the combination of tall necks and decorated bodies with red or red-and-blue-painted bodies. Vessels 4 and 5 are the only ones with blue-painted bodies. Vessels 5 and 3 are the only ones with green paint. If we arrange these vessels so that each feature has a continuous distribution, then the sequence is 1, 2, 4, 5, 3. This can be shown graphically in a matrix (Table 1–1).

TABLE 1–1

FEATURE	VESSEL	TIME				
		1	2	4	5	3
Neck decorated		x				
Red paint exclusively		x	x			
Tall neck		x	x	x		
Body painted			x	x	x	x
Red and blue paint			x			
Blue paint in some combinations			x	x		
Short neck					x	x
Blue and green paint					x	
Green paint						x

In this matrix, each feature has a continuous distribution. This fits the assumption underlying seriational techniques that change is gradual; other sequences do not fulfill this condition. There are two ways of increasing the reliability of such a seriation. One is to examine many more features on the bottles—for example, the kinds of painted designs that occur or the differences in shape and proportion that exist—and to include these observations in the matrix. The other is to expand the size of the sample, so that 10, 50, or 100 bottles from the same local area are examined instead of 5. Of course outside information is still needed to determine the chronological order of the sequence.

REFERENCES

Cowgill, George L. (1972). Models, methods and techniques for seriation. In David L. Clarke (Ed.), *Models in archaeology* (pp. 381–424). London: Methuen & Co..

Deetz, James, & Edwin Dethlefsen. (1965). The Doppler effect and archaeology: A consideration of the spatial aspects of seriation. *Southwestern Journal of Anthropology*, 21(3), 196–206.

Dunnell, Robert C. (1970). Seriation method and its evaluation. *American Antiquity*, 35(3), 305–319.

Marquardt, William H. (1978). Advances in archaeological seriation. In Michael B. Schiffer (Ed.), *Advances in archaeological method and theory* (Vol. 1, pp. 260–314). New York: Academic Press.

Rouse, Irving. (1967). Seriation in archaeology. In Carroll L. Riley & Walter W. Taylor (Eds.), *American historical anthropology: Essays in honor of Leslie Spier* (pp. 153–195). Carbondale: Southern Illinois University Press.

Rowe, John Howland. (1961). Stratigraphy and seriation. *American Antiquity*, 26(pt. 1, 3), 324–330.

Rowe, John Howland. (1962). Worsaae's law and the use of grave lots for archaeological dating. *American Antiquity*, 28(2), 129–137.

Rowe, John Howland. (1972). Review: Winckelmann, by Wolfgang Leppmann. *American Anthropologist*, 74(1–2), 154–156.

THE DATA AND THE PROBLEM

The 12 stirrup spout bottles illustrated in Figure 1–1 (A through L) were excavated in a single cemetery. Radiocarbon measurement on tissues from the individuals buried in the cemetery ranged from 3,800 ± 200 years to 2,600 ± 100 years, suggesting that the cemetery was used over a period of about 1,000 years and that the stirrup bottles from different tombs might have different ages. Each of the tombs excavated contained a single stirrup spout bottle. The tomb containing the vessel illustrated in Figure L had been dug into the shaft of a tomb containing the vessel illustrated in Figure B. The law of superposition, which will be discussed in more detail in Problem 2 says that the materials deposited first are older than those deposited later; consequently, the bottle represented in Figure B is older than the vessel illustrated in Figure L.

A brief description of the chronologically significant features of each of the 12 bottles follows. Keep in mind the old saying that a picture is worth a thousand words and refer to the illustrations.

Figure A Vessel with short, massive conical spout with flanged rim; massive rounded stirrup; convex–curved body with flat bottom; appliqué and punctate decoration over the entire surface of the vessel.

Figure B Vessel with short, massive concave–curved spout with beveled rim; massive rounded stirrup; markedly convex–curved body with flat bottom; vertical bands of zoned punctate decoration alternating with undecorated bands on the body of the vessel; no decoration on either the stirrup or the spout.

Figure C Vessel with short, massive conical spout with flanged rim; massive rounded stirrup; convex–curved body with flat bottom; punctate decoration over the entire body of the vessel; no decoration on the stirrup or the spout.

Figure D Vessel with tall, straight–sided spout, narrow

Figure 1–1

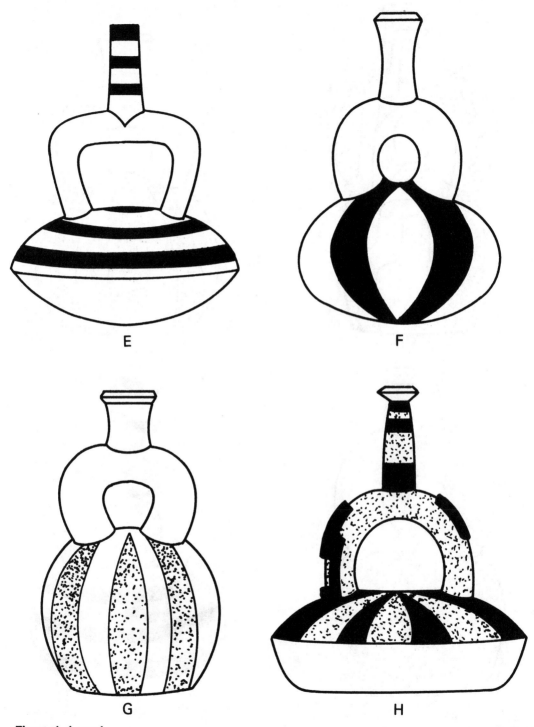

E

F

G

H

Figure 1–1, cont.

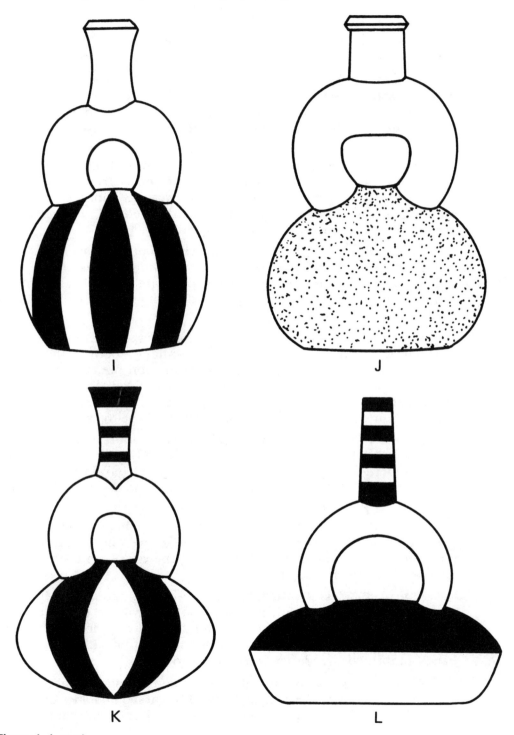

Figure 1–1, cont.

triangular–shaped stirrup; markedly convex–curved body with rounded bottom; circumferential bands of red paint alternating with undecorated bands on the spout and the body; no decoration on the stirrup.

Figure E   Vessel with tall, straight–sided spout; narrow triangular–shaped stirrup; body has a low profile and a marked shoulder angle midheight; circumferential bands of red paint alternating with undecorated bands on the spout and the portion of the body above shoulder angle.

Figure F   Vessel with relatively massive, tall, concave–curved spout with beveled rim; massive rounded stirrup; markedly convex–curved body with rounded bottom; vertical bands of red paint alternating with undecorated bands on the body of the vessel; no decoration on either the stirrup or the spout.

Figure G   Vessel with short massive, rounded concave–curved spout with flanged rim; massive stirrup; markedly convex–curved body with flat bottom; vertical bands of zoned punctate decoration alternating with undecorated bands on the body; no decoration on either the stirrup or the spout.

Figure H   Vessel with tall, narrow conical spout with flanged rim; tall, narrow, rounded stirrups; cupcake–shaped body with marked shoulder angle and flattened bottom; appliqué and punctate decoration on the stirrup; circumferential bands of red paint alternating with bands of punctation on the spout; vertical bands of red paint alternating with bands of punctation on the portion of the body above the shoulder angle.

Figure I   Vessel with relatively massive, tall, concave–curved spout with beveled rim; massive rounded stirrup; markedly convex–curved body with flat bottom; vertical bands of red paint alternating with undecorated bands on the body; no decoration on either the stirrup or the spout.

Figure J   Vessel with massive, straight–sided spout with flat rim; massive rounded stirrup; markedly convex–curved body with bottom; punctate decoration over the entire body of the vessel; no decoration on either the stirrup or the spout.

Figure K   Vessel with tall, concave–curved spout with flat rim; rounded stirrup; markedly convex–curved body with rounded bottom; circumferential bands of red paint alternating with undecorated bands on the spout; vertical red–painted bands alternating with undecorated bands on the body; no decoration on the stirrup.

Figure L   Vessel with tall, narrow conical spout; tall, narrow rounded stirrup; cupcake–shaped body with marked shoulder angle and flattened bottom; circumferential bands of red paint alternating with undecorated bands on the spout, red paint over the entire surface of the body above the shoulder angle; no decoration on the stirrup.

Assuming that the art style used in the cemetery was relatively homogeneous at any given moment and using the seriation technique described earlier, as well as the stratigraphic evidence that is available, arrange the stirrup spout bottles into a chronological sequence, beginning with the earliest vessel and ending with the most recent. Pay attention to the illustrations and to the distribution of features like the proportions of the body, neck, and stirrup, the kind of decoration, where it occurs on the vessels, and whether it is oriented vertically or circumferentially. Is there any vessel that does not seem to fit into the sequence? If so, how do you account for that? Does it have any features that indicate when it was actually made, relative to the other bottles, and where does it belong in the sequence?

DISCUSSION OF THE PROBLEM

The first step in establishing the sequence is to set up a matrix in which as many features as possible have continuous time spans. Significant features include the shape and proportions of the spout, the shape and proportions of the body, the kind of decoration that is used, where the decoration is applied on the vessel, and the orientation of the design field (i.e., whether it is vertical, circumferential, or something else). A quick way to begin setting up the matrix is to examine the differences between the vessels illustrated in Figures B and L. The stratigraphic relationship between the two bottles tells us that vessels with narrow spouts and stirrups, low body profiles, and painted designs are later than those with massive spouts and stirrups, relatively tall body profiles, and punctate decoration.

Four vessels have exclusively punctate decoration; one vessel has a combination of punctate and appliqué decoration; another combines painting and punctation; and six have exclusively painted designs. If we look first at the vessels with punctate decoration, we notice they fall into two groups. One group, composed of Figures C and J, has punctate decoration over the entire body, while the other group, composed of Figures B and G, has vertical bands of punctate decoration alternating with undecorated panels. Since the latter design pattern also occurs on vessels with painted decoration, this suggests that Figures B and G are later than are the two bottles with punctate decoration over their entire bodies. If we look at the form of the rim, we notice that the vessels in Figures C and J have flanged rims, as does one in Figure G. This indicates that flanged rims are older than beveled ones; therefore, Figure G is older than Figure B. If we now look at the proportions of the vessel bodies, we see that Figures J and G have the same globular, flat–bottomed profile, while that of Figure C is proportionately narrower and more similar in form to Figure A. We also notice that Figures A and C share the same massive, conical–shaped spout with flanged rim. This suggests that the sequence of punctate–decorated bottles begins with Figure A, goes through Figures C, J, and G, respectively, and ends with Figure B.

Since painted designs are later than ones with punctation, and the vessel in Figure B is the latest one with punctate decoration, the next group of bottles to look at would be those with painted designs resembling that of the vessel depicted in Figure G. This group includes Figures F, I, and K. The bottles in Figures F and I have beveled rims like the one in Figure B, while the Figure K bottle has a flat rim. The bottle in Figure I also has a flat bottom like the one in Figure G, while the specimens in Figures F and K have rounded bottoms. This indicates that the sequence of vessels with vertical stripes from earliest to most recent, is represented by Figures B, I, F, and K, respectively.

The feature that relates the bottle illustrated in Figure K to the rest of the specimens is the presence of circumferential red–painted bands on the spout. The bottles in Figures K and D share the convex–curved profile of the body and the rounded bottom. This suggests that the bottle in Figure D follows the one illustrated in Figure K. Two features differentiate the Figure D specimen from the one depicted in Figure K: the narrow, straight–sided spout combined with the triangular–shaped stirrup and the presence of circumferential decorative bands on the vessel body. The Figure D bottle shares these features with the vessel illustrated in Figure E. These relationships indicate that the next section of the sequence begins with Figure K, goes through Figures D and E, respectively, and ends with Figure L, which has a striped spout and a body with a marked shoulder angle, as does the Figure E bottle. The time spans of shoulder angles, the spout shape, and the presence of rounded and flattened bottoms also support this sequence.

The bottle represented in Figure H raises a number of questions because it shares features with every other specimen in the sample. This can be explained in at least two different ways. One interpretation is that all the bottles are equivalent in age and that we are observing contemporary variation in the art style. However, this interpretation does not agree with the radiocarbon measurements, suggesting that a cemetery was used for 1,000 years, and the assumption that art style in use at the cemetery was relatively homogeneous at any given time. The other obvious alternative interpretation is that the bottle illustrated in Figure H is an archaism and that the potter who made it selected features from vessels of different ages to create the piece. If this were the case, then the specimen can be no older than the most recent feature on it. Therefore, since the shape of the body is identical to that of the bottle in Figure L, it must belong to the last unit in the seriated sequence.

2

Stratigraphy: Establishing a Sequence from Excavated Archaeological Evidence

THE PRINCIPLES OF STRATIGRAPHY

There are two principles of stratigraphy. The first is called the *law of superposition*, which states that the depositional unit found at the bottom of an undisturbed pile of strata is older than the ones above it. In archaeology, these depositional units would include individual layers, or strata, of habitation refuse, buildings, graves, and pits. The second principle of stratigraphy can be called the *law of strata identified by their contents*, which says that the depositional units at any particular site can be distinguished from one another by differences in the various objects and associations they contain and by differences in the frequencies with which the various cultural materials occur (Rowe 1961: 324).

The first stratigraphic principle allows us to determine the sequence in which cultural assemblages occur in any given locality; the second principle allows us to determine what occurred in the sequence and provides us with a way of correlating or establishing the contemporaneity of cultural assemblages from different localities. These principles were formulated by geologists during the 18th century and were borrowed by archaeologists after they were already established and being used in the earth sciences (Harris 1975, 1979).[1]

1. The principles of stratigraphy play exceedingly important roles in archaeological interpretation. Johann Gottlob Lehmann clearly stated the law of superposition, including its temporal implications, in 1756; the principle was apparently applied first in archaeology by Thomas Jefferson in his *Notes on the State of Virginia*, the second edition of which was published in 1787. The law of content dissimilarity, or strata identified by their contents, was worked out by William Smith in 1796. Its earliest application in archaeology seems to have been in the review of a book dealing with the Swiss Lake Dwellers that was written by Georg Christian Friedrich Lisch and published in 1847 (Rowe 1961: 324).

To establish a sequence from excavated archaeological evidence, it is essential to apply both stratigraphic principles at the same time. Noticing that superposition occurs among the depositional units at a particular site has little archaeological significance unless the contrasts in their cultural contents are also observed. If no differences between the cultural contents of two successive depositional units can be observed, then the archaeologists must treat the contents of the units as if they were contemporary with one another, even though there is evidence that one unit is, in fact, later than another. The law of superposition provides information only about the sequence of deposition at a particular locality. Differences in the contents of the various depositional units make it possible to interpret their sequence as a sequence of cultural assemblages (Rowe 1961: 324).

There are no exceptions to the law of superposition; it has universal application. However, four situations can affect the order of deposition at a given site so that it might not reflect the real archaeological sequence of the locality. First, *mixing* occurs when a digging operation turns dirt over and leaves it in place, so that the contents of two or more depositional units occur in the deposit created by the digging. Second, filling occurs when a depositional unit is laid down to alter the original level of the ground; this kind of depositional unit may contain old materials. Third, *collection* involves the acquisition and reuse of ancient objects, such as jewelry, pottery vessels, grinding stones, or tools. Fourth, the occurrence of *unconformities*, or temporal breaks, in the stratigraphic sequence of an excavation or site results from a change that caused deposition to cease for an indeterminate time span in that particular locality (Dunbar & Rodgers 1957: 116–127; Rowe 1961: 324–326).

REFERENCES

Dunbar, Carl O., & John Rodgers. (1957). *Principles of stratigraphy.* New York: Wiley.

Harris, Edward C. (1975). The stratigraphic sequence: A question of time. *World Archaeology, 7*(1), 109–121.

Harris, Edward C. (1979). The law of archaeological stratigraphy. *World Archaeology, 11*(1), 111–117.

Rowe, John H. (1961). Stratigraphy and seriation. *American Antiquity, 26*(1), 324–330.

THE DATA AND THE PROBLEM

One way in which archaeologists present visual records of the evidence they uncover is to draw raw profiles of the series of strata that were laid down through time and were exposed during the course of their excavations. Ideally, the profile of each wall, or face, should be illustrated; however, for various reasons, this is rarely the case. Such a profile—the north wall of an excavation—is illustrated in Figure 2–1, and each of the exposed strata is identified with a letter. It is useful to read these profiles from the bottom up. The archaeologist's uncertainty at the time of the excavation about the correct chronological sequence of events around the wall in the middle of the profile is indicated by the designation of strata on one side of the wall with one set of letters (e.g., Stratum I); and those on the other side of the wall with a second set (e.g., Stratum I'). Such designations do not indicate that the strata on the two sides of the wall are contemporary with each other, but rather that they were encountered at roughly the same time during the excavation of this particular block of earth.

The contents of each excavation unit are described separately to ensure that the archaeological associations occurring in each are preserved. The descriptions of the contents of each excavation unit, or stratum, that follow are admittedly inadequate because they contain information only about pottery styles, stone tools, and burial types. The reason for the emphasis in the descriptions is purely for the purpose of the questions to be examined in this section. The reason for this focus on pottery and stone tools is that, when they occur at archaeological sites, they are usually among the most abundant kinds of evidence found; consequently, changes in pottery styles and stone tool types are used to define cultural sequences and to correlate materials found in one area with those that have been discovered in another.

The following descriptions give information about the chronologically significant features that occur in each of the excavated strata.

Stratum A   Red-painted pottery; bottles with red-painted surfaces; shaft tomb with child burial in a vessel with red-painted interior and exterior surfaces.

Stratum B   Pottery with circumferential red-painted stripes; bottles with shoulder angles and tapering spouts found throughout the habitation refuse composing the stratum; pit with extended burial dug from the middle of the stratum; burial is associated with one bowl with circumferential red-painted bands and one bowl with punctate and applique decoration.

Stratum C   Fiber-tempered pottery with circumferential red-painted stripes; straight-sided bottle spouts; bottles with undecorated triangular-shaped stirrups.

Stratum D   Sand-tempered pottery with circumferential red-painted stripes; straight-sided bottle spouts; bottles with undecorated triangular-shaped stirrups.

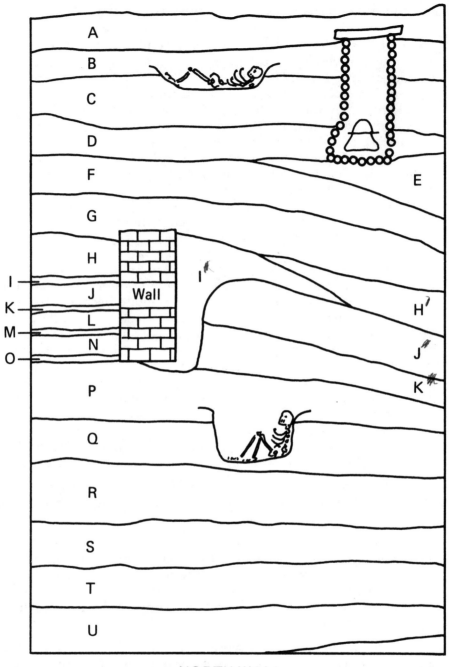

A

B

C

D

F

E

G

H

I

J

Wall

I

K

L

H⁷

M

N

J

O

K

P

Q

R

S

T

U

NORTH WALL

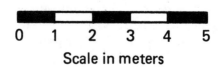

0 1 2 3 4 5

Scale in meters

Figure 2–1

Stratum E   Culturally sterile layer composed of wind-blown sand.

Stratum F   Red-painted pottery; bottles with circumferential red-painted bands on concave-curved spouts.

Stratum G   Pottery with red-painted bands; bottles with rounded bottoms; concave-curved bottle spouts with beveled rims.

Stratum H   (left of wall). Pottery with red-painted bands; bottles with rounded bottoms; concave-curved bottle spouts with beveled rims.

Stratum H'   (right of wall). Pottery with red-painted bands; concave-curved bottle spouts with beveled rims; bottles with flat bottoms.

Stratum I   (left of wall). Horizontal cement layer without cultural remains.

Stratum I'   (right of wall). Pottery with vertical bands of zoned punctate decoration; pottery with punctate decoration; flanged bottle rims; beveled bottle rims.

Stratum J   (left of wall). Green-red-and-blue-painted pottery.

Stratum J'   (right of wall). Pottery with vertical bands of zoned punctate decoration; beveled bottle rims.

Stratum K   (left of wall). Horizontal cement layer without cultural remains.

Stratum K'   (right of wall). Pottery with punctate decoration.

Stratum L   (left of wall). Green-red-and-blue-painted pottery.

Stratum M   (left of wall). Horizontal cement layer without cultural remains.

Stratum N   (left of wall). Pottery with red-painted bands; concave-curved bottle spouts with beveled rims.

Stratum O   (left of wall). Horizontal cement layer without cultural remains.

Stratum P   Pottery with punctate decoration; conical bottle spouts with flanged rims; pit with flexed burial dug from the lower part of the layer.

Stratum Q   Pottery with punctate and appliqué decoration, fragments of conical bottle spouts with flanged rims, single-warp woven cotton textiles.

Stratum R   Undecorated pottery, paired-warp woven cotton textiles, triangular-shaped obsidian spearheads.

Stratum S   Undecorated pottery, paired-warp twined cotton textiles, and triangular-shaped obsidian spearheads.

Stratum T   Paired-warp twined cotton textiles, single-piece shell fishhooks, triangular-shaped obsidian projectile points, grinding stones.

Stratum U   Leaf-shaped Canario projectile points, percussion-flaked choppers, grinding stones.

Using both principles of stratigraphy, as well as the assumption that stylistic change is gradual, what is the most detailed archaeological sequence that can be established from the evidence? Is there any evidence for the occurrence of mixing, filling, collecting, or unconformities? If so, what is the evidence, and where does it occur in the excavation? What was the relationship of the wall with respect to the ground level at the time it was built? What are the relative ages of the depositional units on the right side of the wall compared with those on the left side? Which strata bracket is the construction of the wall? What is the sequence of burial types encountered in the excavation? Does the stratigraphy confirm the seriation of bottles in Problem 1? Compare the rates of change in the cloth-making, stoneworking, and pottery technologies.

DISCUSSION OF THE PROBLEM

The first step in establishing the sequence from the earliest to the most recent archaeological assemblage in the excavation is to apply two principles of stratigraphy. For example, the law of superposition tells us that Stratum U is earlier than Stratum T. When the contents of the strata are compared, we notice a contrast between them: Stratum U contains Leaf-shaped Canario points and percussion-flaked choppers; Stratum T contains paired-warp twined cotton textiles, single-piece shell fishhooks, and triangular projectile points. This difference can be used to define two cultural units—an earlier one with Canario projectile points and a later one with paired-warped twined textiles, shell fishhooks, and triangular-shaped points. Strata S and R also contain the same kind of spearheads that occurs in Stratum T. In addition, they contain pottery, which distinguishes them from Stratum T and different kinds of paired-warp textiles—twined in the earlier layer and woven in the later—which distinguishes them from each other. These differences can be used to establish third and fourth cultural units, the first of which is defined by the presence of undecorated pottery and paired-warp twined textiles and the latter by the presence of undecorated pottery and paired-warp woven textiles. In this situation, it is clear that cloth-making technology was changing more rapidly than the kinds of spearheads that were being made during the time when Strata T to R were deposited. Also, there is a shift in the criteria that can be used to define cultural units during this time. Stone tools are used to define the units from Stratum U, stone tools and textile technology are the basis for defining Stratum T, while pottery and textile technologies become the important diagnostic features for Strata S and R. This situation occurs again in Strata D and C, where the type of temper inclusion added to the clay becomes the chronologically significant feature.

The stratigraphic situation and its interpretation are relatively straightforward until the events that occur around the construction of the wall, which is bracketed in time between Stratum P and Stratum G. The most important questions here are concerned with the relative age of the depositional units on the left and right sides of the wall. Are they the same age, or are the units on one side of the wall older than those on the other? The principles of stratigraphy do not provide us with clear answers to these questions; consequently, we must use a seriational technique to answer them.

The idea that styles change gradually has several corollaries. One is that style features have continuous distributions in time; another is that styles that share a large number of features with one another are closer in age than are those that share only a few features or none at all. When a seriation technique is used, we see that the contents of Strata P and K' are identical and therefore form a single cultural unit. We also observe that Strata N and H' also have identical contents as do Strata H and G. This shows that the depositional units on the left side of the wall are more recent than are those on the right side. The stratigraphic situation and its interpretation become relatively clear again after Stratum G.

Conditions that obscure the order of deposition at an archaeological site occur frequently in the vicinity of architecture and burials, where earth is dug up and/or moved. We can gain additional information about the construction of the wall when the contents of Stratum I' are examined and contrasted with those of Strata J' and K'. The contents of Stratum I' can be viewed as a mixture of those from Strata J' and K'. If this is correct, then someone dug a hole from the top of Stratum J' to the bottom of Stratum K', mixed the dirt and debris from the two layers in the same pile, built the wall of a subterranean or semisubterranean structure, and then covered the exposed outside surface with the dirt and debris he or she had previously dug up. Stratum I' certainly is an example of mixing and probably of filling as well. Stratum E, a culturally sterile layer of sand, might also be an example of filling in order to level the land surface; however, the reasons why this might have been done are not apparent from the evidence available from excavation.

The best evidence for collecting occurs in the pottery associated with the extended burial in Stratum B, where a pottery bowl with punctate and appliqué decoration is a unique specimen in an assemblage composed entirely of pottery with red-painted stripes. In other words, it is intrusive. The intrusion could be the result of trade or some other form of exchange; however, the fact that punctate and applique pottery occurred earlier in Stratum R suggests that the vessel might have been collected locally. The striking difference between the contents of Strata U and T suggests that there may be an unconformity between the two layers, even though the two beds are parallel and the contact is a simple bedding plane.

Bottles with punctate and applique decoration and flanged rims, resembling 1A, are found in Stratum Q; bottles with punctate decoration and flanged rims, resembling 1C, are found in Stratum P; bottles with flanged rims and vertical bands of zoned punctation, like 1G, occur in Stratum J'; bottles with red-painted vertical bands and concave-curved spouts with beveled rims, like the one in 1F, occur in Strata G and H; bottles with rounded bottoms and circumferential red-painted stripes on concave-curved spouts, like 1K, are found in Stratum F; bottles with circumferential red-painted stripes, like those in 1D, occur in Stratum D; bottles with shoulder angles and tapering spouts, like those in 1E, occur in Stratum B; and bottles with red-painted surfaces, like 1L, are found in Stratum A.

Constructing
a Regional Chronology

REGIONAL ARCHAEOLOGICAL RESEARCH

Archaeological research is carried out most commonly on a regional basis. That is, one or more archaeologists undertake extensive investigations in a single region—a river valley, an intermontane basin, the top of a large mesa—that is located in and forms a part of a larger geographical area, such as the Near East or the American Southwest. These investigations generally involve some combination of systematic exploration to locate the archaeological sites that still exist in the region and excavation at a limited number of sites that have been selected for various reasons for more intensive study. Perhaps the most important result of this kind of research project is that archaeological evidence is available from a relatively large number of sites. This enhances the archaeologists' perspective; it permits viewing and interpreting the remains from any given site in terms of what was happening elsewhere in the region.

CHRONOLOGICAL RELATIONSHIPS

One of the first things that must be established with this kind of research is the chronological relationships of the various sites and excavated assemblages. Archaeologists must determine which sites are the oldest, which are the most recent, and which are contemporary with one another, before making any statements about social development in the region. To do this, they will use both principles of stratigraphy in combination with seriational arguments to place the various sites and assemblages in their proper chronological order, beginning with the earliest ones and ending with the most recent. The purpose is to establish a relative sequence based on the objects and associations that occur at the different sites.

For example, suppose that the archaeologists found and excavated a site with three distinct strata. The archaeological assemblage from the bottom stratum contained gourd bowls, twined cotton shirts, thorn fishhooks, and disc-shaped beads. The middle stratum at the site was culturally sterile. The assemblage in the top stratum contained red-painted pottery bowls, woven cotton shirts, and shell fishhooks. On the basis of the contrasts between the contents of the assemblages and the evidence for superposition, the archaeologists can define a sequence composed of two units. Suppose that a second site was excavated in a nearby locality situated in the same kind of environmental zone. It contained three strata. The assemblage from the bottom stratum contain twined cotton shirts, thorn fishhooks, stone bowls, and tubular beads. The assemblage from the middle stratum was composed of stone bowls, tubular beads, undecorated pottery bowls, and woven cotton shirts. The most recent assemblage at the site contained red-painted pottery bowls, woven cotton shirts, and shell fishhooks. A matrix of the evidence described appears as Table 3–1.

Table 3–1

			Time		
Assemblage Feature	*1-bottom*	*2-bottom*	*2-middle*	*2-top*	*1-top*
Gourd bowls	x				
Disc-shaped beads	x				
Twined cotton shirts	x	x			
Thorn fishhooks	x	x			
Stone bowls		x	x		
Tubular beads		x	x		
Woven cotton shirts			x	x	x
Pottery bowls			x	x	x
Undecorated			x		
Red-painted				x	x
Shell fishhooks				x	x

The arrangement of the assemblages in the matrix is supported by the evidence of superposition that is available and by a seriational argument in which all the chronologically significant features have continuous times spans. It is also clear that two assemblages—those from the top stratum at both sites—have identical contents and, therefore, must be treated as if they were contemporary with one another. This does not mean that they are precisely equivalent in age, but only that they must be assigned to the same arbitrary division of time, or *period*, because no significant differences can be recognized in their contents. Depending on the amounts of time that passed while they were being deposited and by the duration of the period to which they are being assigned, the two assemblages may, in fact, have the same age, overlap in time, or have different ages. If the length of the period is short and their durations in time are brief, then there is a higher probability the assemblages are more nearly equivalent in age (Patterson 1963).

Contemporary archaeological assemblages from the same region share distinctive features that distinguish them from other assemblages are said to belong to the same cultural unit, or *phase* (Willey & Phillips 1958: 22–24). Suppose that the red-painted bowls found in the top stratum at each of the two excavated sites mentioned are chronologically very significant in the region and that they are also found at other sites in different localities and environmental zones. At one site they occur in shaft and chamber tombs; at another they are found in storage pits situated in the fortified portions of a farming settlement; at a third they are associated with food remains in a garbage dump. Given the different associations of contemporaneity in which this particular vessel occurs, the archaeologists can infer a great deal about the behavior of the people who used it (Patterson 1993).

Two problems can occur and make it difficult to establish detailed, regional chronologies. These involve the nature of the samples of archaeological evidence from the different sites in the region and the time spans that are represented by the various excavated assemblages and surface collections from these sites. The sample from any given site be inadequate because it does not reflect what actually occurs there. At least three factors can affect the reliability of archaeological samples: (1) differential site preservation and destruction in the region, (2) differences in the preservation conditions that exist among the various sites, and (3) human judgment or error—for example, the site was not located in the survey, the archaeologist spent too little time studying an extensive and/or deep site, or the excavations, if any, were too few and located in the wrong parts of the site. The durations in time represented by the various excavated assemblages and surface collections can vary significantly from one site to another in a particular region. For instance, the surface collection from one site may contain objects that were deposited over a period of 2,000 or 3,000 years and have features that are diagnostic of several different phases that have been defined elsewhere in the region on the basis of evidence—associations of contemporaneity—with more limited time spans.

REFERENCES

Patterson, Thomas C. (1963). Contemporaneity and cross-dating in archaeological interpretation. *American Antiquity*, 28(3), 389–392.

Patterson, Thomas C. (1993). *Archaeology: The historical development of civilizations*, 2nd ed. Englewood Cliffs, NJ: Prentice Hall.

Willey, Gordon R., & Philip Phillips. (1958). *Method and theory in American archaeology*. Chicago: University of Chicago Press.

THE DATA AND THE PROBLEM

The locations of 17 archaeological sites in a region are shown in the map in Figure 3–1. The cultural remains and stratigraphic information from the sites are as follows.

Site 1   Stratified site. Lower stratum contains single-warp twined cotton textiles, single-piece shell fishhooks, Encanto projectile points, and grinding stones. Upper stratum contains paired-warp twined cotton textiles, rocker milling stones, and single-piece shell fishhooks.

Site 2   Paired-warp twined cotton textiles, single-piece fishhooks, and stone-faced terraces.

Site 3   Looped grass textiles, grinding stone, Canario projectile points, and remains of a circular thatched house.

Site 4   Stratified site. Lower stratum contains single-warp twined cotton textiles, grinding stones, and single-piece shell fishhooks. Upper stratum contains paired-warp twined cotton textiles, rocker milling stones, and single-piece shell fishhooks.

Site 5   Adobe-covered stone-walled apartment house and storage complex associated with paired-warp twined cotton textiles, single-piece shell fishhooks, and stone-faced terraces.

Site 6   Canario projectile points, grinding stones, stone scrapers, and the remains of a circular thatched house.

Site 7   Encanto projectile points, single-warp twined cotton textiles, and grinding stones.

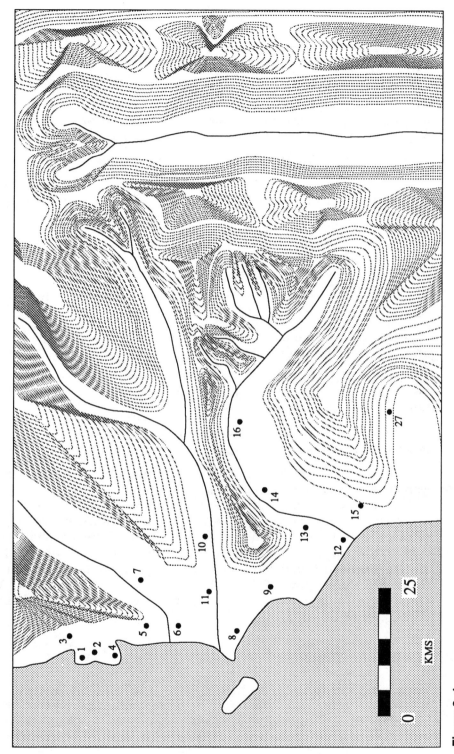

Figure 3–1

Site 8 Paired-warp twined cotton textiles and single-piece shell fishhooks.

Site 9 Stratified site. Lower stratum contains paired-warp twined cotton textiles, single-piece shell fishhooks, and rocker milling stone fragments. Upper stratum contains paired-warp woven cotton textiles, single-piece shell fishhooks, and undecorated pottery.

Site 10 Stone-faced terraces, rectangular houses with stone walls, and rocker milling stone fragments.

Site 11 Adobe-covered, stone-walled structure that was destroyed 30 years ago to build a municipal jail. Archaeologists who visited the site state that the architecture resembled that of Site 5.

Site 12 Adobe-covered stone-walled houses on stone-faced terrace and rocker milling stone fragments.

Site 13 Small stone-walled apartment house and storage complex, paired-warp twined cotton textiles, and rocker milling stones.

Site 14 Stone-faced terraces, stone-walled rectangular houses, and rocker milling stone fragments.

Site 15 Canario projectile points, semisubterranean circular houses with thatched walls and whalebone wall supports, extended burials, and thorn fishhooks.

Site 16 Stone-walled houses on stone-faced terraces and rocker milling stone fragments.

Site 27 Canario projectile points, Encanto projectile points, grinding stones, and undecorated pottery.

Using both principles of stratigraphy, as well as seriational arguments, assign each assemblage to a phase, establish the sequence of phases, and discuss the distinctive features of each phase in the region. How many phases are represented at the various sites, and what are the diagnostic features of each? Is there any site that does not seem to fit into the sequence? If so, how do you account for that? What chronological relationships do these sites have with the excavated site described in Problem 2?

DISCUSSION OF THE PROBLEM

The easiest way to approach this problem is to look first for contrasts in the cultural contents of the strata at sites where superposition occurs. There are three stratified sites in the region Sites 1, 4, and 9. At each site, the contents of the lower stratum have features that differ from those of the upper stratum. The assemblages from the lower strata at Sites 1 and 4 share single-warp twined cotton textiles and grinding stones, which distinguish them from the upper strata at the sites. The upper strata at Sites 1 and 4 and the lower stratum from Site 9 contain paired-warp twined cotton textiles and rocker milling stones, which distinguish these assemblages from other units at the same sites. The upper stratum of Site 9 contains paired-warp woven cotton textiles and undecorated pottery, which, in turn, distinguish it from the earlier unit at that site. At this point, we have a sequence composed of three chronologically distinct phases, each of which has certain diagnostic features.

The next step is to examine the remainder of the sites in the region to determine whether any of them share features with the three phases defined at the stratified site. At this point, we notice that Site 7 shares three features with the lower stratum of Site 1—single-warp twined cotton textiles, grinding stones, and Encanto projectile points—and two features with the lower stratum of Site 4—single-warp twined cotton textiles and grinding stones. Since no significant features distinguish it from the other two assemblages, we must treat them as if they were contemporary with one another. Therefore, Site 7 is contemporary with the assemblages from the lower strata of Sites 1 and 4.

Continuing this process of interpretation, we observe that paired-warp twined cotton textiles, which occur in the upper strata at Sites 1 and 4 and in the lower stratum of Site 9 also occur in Sites 2, 5, 8, and 13. Rocker milling stones, which are also characteristic of this cultural unit, occur in Sites 10, 12, 13, 14, and 16. Stone architecture—be it adobe-covered stone walls, rectangular stone-walled houses, or stone-faced terraces—is found at Sites 2, 5, 10, 11, 12, 13, 14, and 16. These features—paired-warp twined cotton textiles, rocker milling stones, and stone architecture—always occur in some combination with one another. Consequently, all assemblages mentioned in this paragraph belong to the same phase.

The assemblages from Sites 3, 6, and 15 share two features that distinguish them from other units found at the other sites: Canario projectile points and some sort of circular thatched house. Two of the assemblages, those from Sites 6 and 15, have unique features: stone scrapers at the first and thorn fishhooks and extended burials at the latter. As a phase, they share projectile points and grinding stones with the assemblages from Site 7 and the lower strata from Sites 1 and 4. A seriational argument based on this fact would suggest that this phase is the earliest in a four-phase sequence for the region and that the differences between the three assemblages assigned to this unit are due to factors other than time.

The collection from Site 27 contains features that are characteristic of three of the units defined elsewhere in the region on the basis of stratigraphic information or associations of contemporaneity in what appear to be single-occupation sites. The data from this site are inadequate for defining cultural units, since they are mixed; however, they suggest that the site was occupied or used either continuously or sporadically during the period when the first two phases were in use; it was abandoned during the time of the third phase and was reused during the time of the fourth phase.

The presence of Canario projectile points in Stratum T relates that excavation unit to the earliest phase, the one defined by the materials found at Sites 3, 6, and 15. The second phase—defined by the single-warp twined textiles and other materials from the lower layers of Sites 1 and 4 and from Site 7—was not represented at the excavation described in Problem 2. The paired-warp twined cotton textiles of the third phase from Sites 1 upper, 4 upper, 2, 5, 8, 9 lower, 10, 11, 12, 13, 14, and 16 occur in Stratas T and S; the absence of undecorated pottery at any of the sites located in the region suggests that Phase 3 is most likely contemporary with the assemblage from Stratum T. The paired-warp woven textiles and undecorated pottery found in the Phase 4 assemblage from the upper layer of Site 9 indicate that it is contemporary with the materials from Stratum R.

Technical Divisions of Labor and Social Reproduction

People work to satisfy their needs and to ensure the continued existence of the group to which they belong. This means they engage in activities—the provisioning of food, tools, and emotional support, for instance—that occur on a daily basis and restore their capacity for work; they participate in routines that ensure the biological reproduction of life and demographic replacement; and they take part in practices that reproduce or modify the necessary conditions and social relations that allow the communities to persist through time (Lee 1990: 227–228).

This work is characterized by two inseparable elements. One is the labor process itself in which human beings, using definite tools and techniques, expend energy to procure raw materials and to transform them into useful goods. The other involves the relationships that exist among the different individuals who participate in one way or another in the labor process; these are called the relations of production. The labor process always takes place in concrete, historical, specific circumstances, where definite relationships exist among the individuals who are involved in the process of production.

In all societies, production and consumption are connected processes. They are also continuous and perpetually repeated, since no society can cease to consume. Production is necessary for the maintenance of life. There is a close, obvious relationship among production, consumption, and the ways in which useful objects are distributed in the society—that is, how useful items get from the individuals who make them to those who ultimately use or consume them. At the same time, the cultural forms that structure production and consumption also reproduce, re-create, or set up the conditions under which production can continue to take place.

In producing a useful good, members of a society take a raw material and shape it with tools or implements, which were made earlier from other raw materials, to satisfy some culturally defined need. This useful object may be the product of the activity of one individual working alone or of a number of individuals working simultaneously or sequentially as the raw material is transformed step by step into something with use and value. The good may be used by its producer; it may be divided, according to tradition, among all the individuals who were involved in the production process; or it may be shared with other individuals who were not involved directly in the production process. The rules of distribution that prevail in a particular society determine not only who has access to the useful goods produced, but also how much they are entitled to (Marx 1973: 83–100).

In all societies, people divide up the tasks that have to be performed to satisfy their needs. That is, there is a division of labor. Labor can be divided or segmented in several ways. One involves dividing the tasks into different sectors—such as agriculture, mining, or fishing—so that individuals specialize to a greater or lesser extent in the work activities associated with one sphere of production and not others. A second divides a particular productive process into a series of distinct tasks, each of which is performed by a different worker; this is what happens in assembly-line production in modern industrial societies. Consequently, the individuals involved in the production of one useful good may not participate in the production of some of the other goods they consume. However, in some societies, the distinction between producers and nonproducers, which describes the connections between given individuals in relation to a particular productive activity, disappears when the perspective is broadened to include a number of different activities (Leacock 1982: 159; Siskind 1978).

There are two major kinds of labor processes. One involves the laborer who works alone to transform some raw material into a useful object. The other is a cooperative process in which a number of workers participate in the production of a useful object; each of the workers may perform the same set of tasks, or each may carry out a specific task that corresponds to one part of the productive process and reflects a technical division of labor. The segmentation of work may be rigidly or loosely organized (Harnecker 1969).

Technical divisions are also culturally constructed. That is, work is structured by the age, gender, ethnic, and racial differences that were understood to exist in the historically specific community being investigated. These are complex categories. For example, gender differences refer to the ways in which the sexual differences that are perceived to be natural are constructed. Such constructions have two levels. One level is concerned with what is understood to be natural: Biology, occupation, sexual preference, age, and the possession of female essence are only a few of the criteria mentioned in the ethnographic and historical literature. The other level attaches significance to the sexual differences that have been selected to constitute men, women, or other genders in a particular society. Ethnicity and race, if these categories existed, have similarly complex constructions and linkages with social production and reproduction.

In recent years, physical anthropologists and archaeologists have become increasingly aware that the consequences of work and everyday life are often inscribed in the bodies of the individuals who perform particular tasks (Larsen 1987). For example, men and women who frequently swim and dive in cold water often have lesions or exostoses on their ear bones; those who carry heavy loads often have spines with wedge-shaped vertebra resulting from compressed or collapsed intervertebral discs; miners have high incidence of black lung and other respiratory ailments; stoneworkers often exhibit arthritis in their wrists as well as smashed fingers; and the incisors and canines of men and women who use their teeth to prepare construction materials from animal sinew or plant remains are often grooved and chipped as a result.

The process of production is a problem of considerable theoretical importance to archaeologists. How are production, circulation, distribution, and consumption organized in the ancient society being investigated? How is the population segmented into producers, on the one hand, and consumers, on the other? How does this segmentation change, if at all, when different useful goods are produced? What patterns of overlap exist between the membership of production units and consumption units? Since the relationship between producer and consumer is a social—and not necessarily a biological—one, how is it expressed in that society? And where do the production and consumption of different useful goods take place?

REFERENCES

Harnecker, Marta. (1969). *Los conceptos elementales del materialismo historico*. Mexico: Siglo Veintiano (See especially production and the relations of production, pp. 19–56.)

Larsen, Clark S. (1987). Bioarchaeological interpretations of subsistence economy and behavior from human skeletal remains. In Michael B. Schiffer (Ed.), *Advances in archaeological method and theory* (Vol. 10, pp. 339–445). San Diego: Academic Press.

Leacock, Eleanor B. (1982). Relations of production in band society. In Eleanor Leacock & Richard Lee (Eds.), *Politics and history in band societies* (pp. 159–170). Cambridge: Cambridge University Press.

Lee, Richard B. (1990). Primitive communism and inequality. In Steadman Upham (Ed.), *The evolution of political systems: Sociopolitics in small-scale sedentary societies* (pp. 225–247). Cambridge: Cambridge University Press.

Marx, Karl. (1973). *Grundrisse: Introduction to the critique of political economy.* Trans. Martin Nicolaus. New York: Vintage Books.

Siskind, Janet. (1978). Kinship and modes of production. *American Anthropologist*, 80(4), 860–872.

THE DATA AND THE PROBLEM

After the regional chronology described in Problem 3 was established, more extensive excavations were conducted in four of the sites shown in Figure 4-1. The following are summaries of the excavation data relevant for this problem.

Site 1: Upper stratum   This settlement, which had an estimated population of 50 to 100 people, is located on a hillside overlooking rocky headlands and a small beach. The limited excavations revealed the remains of 27 stone-lined pithouses, quite uniform in size, with floor areas averaging about 80 by 170 centimeters and two food-preparation areas with hearths and four clay-lined storage pits containing the identifiable remains of two species of wild fruits, potatoes, sweet potatoes, chili peppers, peanuts, squash, and avocados. Agricultural production would have been impossible given the absence of fresh water near the settlement; the nearest spring was located 12 kilometers east of the village.

The excavations also yielded 38 burials. Twenty were infants and juveniles, each of which was interred in a pit, covered with red ocher, and associated with a quartz crystal and necklace composed of five to ten beads made from turquoise, or spondylus shell. There were three adolescent males, five adolescent females, four adult males, and six adult females; all but one of the adults were less than 30 years old. All the adolescent and adult burials, except one 17-year-old female, exhibited exostoses of the ear bones, and all were buried with twined, paired-warp cotton shirts and had thorn and shell fishhooks, cotton fishing line and nets, gourd floats, stone sinkers placed in their graves, and necklaces made of stone or shell beads. A 40-year-old adult male adorned with a shell necklace was interred with a wooden loom, a bone, a needle, a bodkin, spindle whorls, and a ball of cotton yarn.

Site 2   This site is located about 200 meters south of Site 1. Excavations reveal that 1- to 2-meter deep refuse deposits had built up

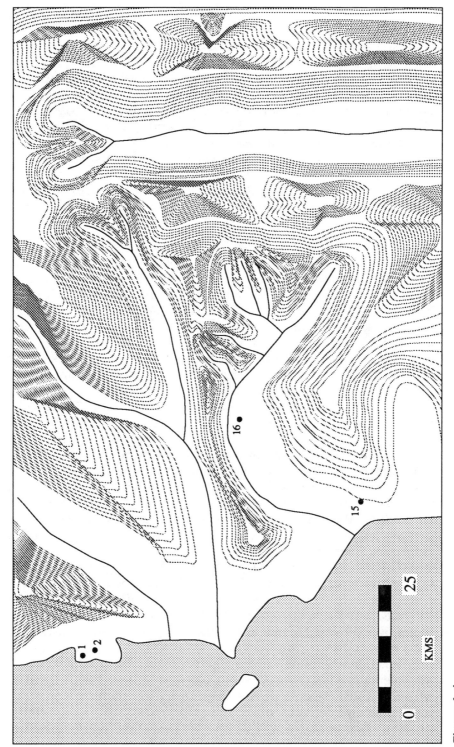

Figure 4–1

against the front edges of a series of 200-meter-long terraces; these were composed enormous quantities of fish scales and eyes from both deep-water and beach species, the carapaces of marine crustaceans, and marine bivalves, many of which had been pried open with thin stone flakes that were strewn throughout the refuse layers. Artifacts were scarce and included broken thorn and shell fishhooks, fragments of casting nets made from cotton, as well as scraps of twined, paired-warp cotton textiles. The surfaces of the terraces were composed a mixture of soil; foliated bedrock, fish scales, broken and scorched marine mollusks, burned driftwood, sedges, and grasses. The construction of the stone terraces required an estimated 1 million person-days of labor.

Site 15   This site is located 6 kilometers from the ocean. Twelve semisubterranean pithouses, averaging 3 meters in diameter, were excavated as were associated refuse deposits. Food was prepared in front houses; dried fish, smoked meat, and edible seaweed were stored in basket-lined pits adjacent to the houses. Refuse deposits indicate that the diet of the inhabitants included deep-water and tidal zone marine mollusks, fish found around rocky points, marine and riverine crustaceans, sea lions, bird eggs, seaweed, deer, wild fruits, and tubers and rhizomes collected from nearby areas of fog vegetation. Bottle gourd fragments were the only indication of possible domesticated plants.

A total of 23 infants and/or juveniles, less than 5 years old, were buried in pits dug into the floors of the houses. Four houses had one burial pit; eight houses had two pits; and one had three pits. The floors were replastered and the houses continued to be occupied. Adolescents and adults were buried in pits adjacent to each house. A total of 50 burials—23 adolescents and 27 adults—were uncovered. Seven houses were associated with three burials; two with four burials; and one with six burials. Males and females were found at each house. Each of the burials—infants, children, adolescents, and adults—was wrapped in a twined mat made reeds and sedge fibers.

The infants and juvenile males and females were buried with bone beads and quartz crystals. Each of the 12 adolescent and 10 adult males, under 35 years of age, had exostoses on their ear bones and was interred with thorn fishhooks, stone sinkers, and net bags. The three males over 35 years of age also exhibited lesions on their ear bones and grooves worn in their incisors and canines; each was interred with thorn needles, bone bodkins, and sedge cordage. The 9 adolescent and 12 adult females less than 35 years old were interred with spears tipped with Canario projectile points, digging sticks, hammerstones, and net bags. The two females older than 35 years were buried with thorn needles, bone bodkins, and sedge cordage. The adult females exhibited varying degrees of arthritis in one or both wrists, and five had one or more broken or smashed fingers.

Site 16   This settlement overlooked the seasonally inundated floodplain of a small river. Excavations uncovered the remains of two large storage pits filled with raw cotton and eight houses with plastered stone walls; the domestic structures were remarkably uniform in size, averaging about 3 by 5 meters. Each had a hearth and several storage pits adjacent to the entrance. The clay-lined storage pits contained the remains of domesticated sweet potatoes, peanuts, potatoes, chili peppers, and squash. Domestic refuse behind each house contained marine fish, deer, and bird bones; squash stems, avocado pits, lucuma shells, pacae pods, marine mollusks, the carapaces of marine and riverine crustaceans, cotton seeds, and ocas, which grow at much higher elevations.

The excavations also yielded 40 burials. Twenty were infants and juveniles, each of which was interred in a pit beneath the house floors, which were then plastered over. Each was covered with red ocher and was associated with a quartz crystal and necklace composed of 5 to 10 turquoise, anthracite, or spondylus shell beads. Five adolescent males, five adolescent females, six adult males, and four adult females were interred in a cemetery adjacent to a large platform mound; they were also adorned with stone and shell-beaded necklaces. All but three of the adults were less than 30 years old. All of the adults had wedged-shaped vertebra resulting from compressed or flattened intervertebral discs. Only two adult males exhibited exostoses of their inner ear bones. Five adult women showed signs of arthritis in their wrists and one had a smashed finger; all five were interred with small pieces of unworked turquoise, anthracite coal, and spondylus shell and lapidary's tool kits composed of sandstone files and drills, hardwood saws, and sets of hammerstones made from granodiorite river cobbles of different weights. All adolescents and adults, both male and female, were buried with twined, paired-warp cotton shirts and had digging sticks with stone weights and net bags made from cotton. The adolescents, both male and female, had spears tipped with triangular-shaped obsidian projectile points placed in their graves. Adults older than 30 years were interred with spindle whorls, looms, bone bodkins, bone needles, and balls of cotton yarn.

The pyramid required 1.2 million person-days of labor to build; it had a series of large storage pits, some of which contained cotton seeds while gourds were stored in the rest; it was topped by an enclosed structure with a central hearth that yielded burned chili pepper seeds.

To answer the questions below, it is necessary to keep in mind the chronological relationships that exist among the various sites—that is, the relationships you established in Problem 3. How were production, consumption, and distribution organized at each settlement? What technical divisions of labor are represented at each? Is there any evidence for gender-linked craft specialization? Is there any evidence for production activities that were structured by the age of the participants? Do the technical divisions of labor change through time and over space? What are the chronological relationships of Sites 1 and 2? What are the real units of appropriation, and do they vary from one settlement to another? What role does intersettlement exchange play? Is there any evidence for matrimonial mobility between settlements? What implications does the construction of the terraces at Site 2 as well as the platform mound at Site 16 have for the mobilization of labor and the organization of the community? What implications might the activities that occurred at it have for the organization of the community?

DISCUSSION OF THE PROBLEM

The earliest community is represented by the settlement at Site 15. Excavations in the habitation refuse deposits indicate that its residents had a subsistence economy dominated by fishing, littoral harvesting, hunting, and foraging; however, there is nothing intrinsic in these activities that tells us how work was organized. The household was the basic production and consumption unit in this settlement, judging by the presence of storage pits near domestic structures and the burials of infants and children beneath the floors of houses that were still being and by the presence of adolescent and adult burials in pits located in close proximity to the domestic structures. The skeletal remains and grave goods indicate that there was a technical division of labor based on age and gender. The remains of adolescent and adult males frequently exhibit exostoses on the inner, while females do not. One circumstance that promotes the growth of these lesions is immersion in water with temperatures below 17.5 degrees celsius. This suggests that adolescent boys and young men engaged in deep-water swimming and diving for mollusks, while girls and women did not. The grave goods suggest that adolescent and adult women foraged, hunted, and made stone tools. The presence of weaving implements in the graves of women and older men indicates that some tasks were age-related rather than gender-specific.

The technical division of labor based on age and gender meant that no individual in the community was able to procure or produce all of the goods essential for life. It necessitated cooperation—sharing the products of one's labor with one or more members of the opposite sex and different generations in return for a portion of the products of their labor. Kinship expresses the linkage between sharing and the division of labor. Each item that was acquired or produced—for example, shellfish or twined mats—potentially moved through a circuit of individuals before it was used or consumed. In this settlement, the circuit through which some subsistence goods moved apparently involved the members of households: their adult men, adult women, and children. Marriage and filiation defined the membership and place of an individual in one of these domestic groups and, given the technical division of labor, determined his or her share of its production.

Households were relatively enduring social groups in the community, judging by the presence of burials beneath house floors and in close proximity to them. The durability of households as social units implies they exhibited developmental cycles reflecting changes over time in their size, composition, and organization. It further suggests that there were also long-term connections between the various households or domestic groups of a village or camp. The small number of people who resided in the settlements—between 25 and 75 individuals at any given moment—meant that the village was too small to be an autonomous, independent demographic entity. It must have been linked by matrimonial mobility as men and women moved between settlements to find suitable mates, and the composition of the various settlements must have mirrored this practice. It also meant that the relations of production and the relations of reproduction operated at different levels. While the real appropriation of nature occurred at the level of the household and perhaps the village, neither level was able to ensure demographic replacement and the continuity of the community. Their social and demographic reproduction was underwritten by relations and practices that operated between, rather than within, the settlements.

Production and its spatial organization were transformed by the time Sites 1, 2, and 16 were occupied and/or used. Sites 1 and 2 were established on the coast near rich fishing grounds. The former was a habitation settlement and the latter was an economically specialized work station where fish and mollusks were dried. However, since agriculture was impossible around the fishing villages, the cultivation of cotton, gourds, and food plants must have been carried out at some distance from them. This suggests that there were economically specialized farming settlements besides the fishing villages. It also indicates that production was organized on a regional basis.

This new territorial organization of production was not merely superimposed on the existing age- and gender-based division of labor characteristic of the earlier community represented at Site 15, nor did it completely supplant and transform that arrangement by creating a new technical division of labor between farming and fishing villages. In the new, economically specialized fishing communities, both men and women engaged in activities taking place around the sea, judging by the fact that both sexes had exostoses on their inner ears. In inland farming settlements, males and females typically lacked exostoses, presumably since both engaged in farming rather than ocean fishing. Thus, while the labor practices in fishing villages and farming hamlets became more differentiated, the work activities of men and women within the same economically specialized settlement converged. However, old people in both farming and fishing settlements continued to sew and weave as their ancestors had, while adolescent males and females in the farming hamlet began to hunt as their female ancestors had generations earlier. Some women who resided at the farming hamlet were also lapidaries and jewelers, judging by the tool kits found in their tombs.

The burials of two males with exostoses at the Site 16 farming hamlet and the 17-year-old female in the fishing village may provide evidence of matrimonial mobility between fishing and farming settlements. The evidence suggests that both men and women of reproductive age moved between the settlements.

The composition of the household consumption units changed during the later phase. In the farming hamlet at Site 16, the household remained the basic unit of appropriation and consumption. In the fishing village at Site 1, the domestic structures were much smaller and food preparation was apparently carried out in communal kitchens that served several households rather than in individual residences.

The relations of production and reproduction that developed in the later community did not replicate those that had existed earlier. They involved instead the elaboration of community-level relations and new forms of articulation with the domestic level, which was composed of the households where the real appropriation of raw materials and their transformation into usable goods still occurred. The community-level relations, previously manifested in the practices of matrimonial mobility, came to link economically specialized settlements composed of households whose members were no longer able to produce all of the materials they consumed given the spatially organized, technical division of labor that had developed in the new kinds of villages. Community-level social relations permitted the inhabitants of the specialized settlements to acquire, on a regular basis, raw materials and goods from distant localities; thus, the adults from the farming hamlets carried agricultural produce and raw cotton to the inhabitants of the fishing villages and returned to their homes with dried fish. The community-level relations of production were also involved in construction projects— building the terraces or the platform mound that outstripped the labor capabilities of a single household or settlement. The pyramid functioned as a storehouse for the cotton and gourds used at the fishing village and the locus of the farming hamlet cemetery. The structure on its summit was an enclosed space where people, possibly from both the fishing and farming hamlets involved in the community labor activities, inhaled the fumes of burning chili peppers on certain occasions.

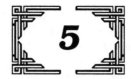

5

Time and Space as Operating Conditions in Production

When the members of a historically specific society engage in work activities to satisfy their needs and to ensure the continued existence of the group, they do so at particular times and particular places. As a result, time and place are important factors in production and in the constitution of the relations of production and reproduction. They are operating conditions that shape when and where production, consumption, and social reproduction take place. However, they are not identical to production and consumption, with the social relations that organize those practices, or with nature itself. These operating conditions are autonomous, interactive, and integral aspects of a society's whole system of production and reproduction (Mészáros 1987).

SEASONAL ACTIVITIES

As a result, archaeologists attempting to reconstruct the life ways of an ancient society are particularly interested in determining the season or seasons of the year when a site was used, the activities that occurred there, and how these practices were organized. They answer the first question—the time of year when a site was used—by relying on several different kinds of evidence. These include the various kinds of information provided by faunal remains, the contents of coprolites (desiccated feces), botanical remains, and the nature of the sediments in which these materials and other associated objects were incorporated (Heizer 1960; Monk 1982).

The use of faunal remains to determine the time of occupation is based on the skeletal development and age at death of the animals recovered as well as their seasonal behavior. Many animal species have marked breeding and birth seasons; consequently, if an immature individual is recovered and its age can be determined from the development of the skeleton, then it is possible to determine the time of year when the animal died or was killed, provided that the time of the birth season of the particular species is known. For example, suppose that a 6-month-old animal was recovered and that this species had a birth season that falls in late April; then, given the age at death, it is clear that the animal died in late October. The two most important techniques for determining the age at death of animals are the development of the skeleton from infant to juvenile to mature individuals of the same species and the pattern of tooth eruption and the sequential replacement of the milk or deciduous teeth by adult ones (Bökönyi 1972; Crabtree 1990; Flannery 1967).

Other aspects of seasonal animal behavior—such as annual growth cycles or fluctuations in the local availability and abundance of particular species due to migration, mating, or hibernation—can also be used to determine the time of year when a site was occupied. Many species, including fish, marine mollusks, and deer, exhibit specific annual growth cycles; for example, deer grow and shed their antlers at particular times of the year, and many marine mollusks add growth rings reflecting alternating periods of growth and dormancy, in much the same way that trees do. Migratory animals—for example, sea lions, reindeer, salmon, or ducks—are found at particular localities only during certain times of the year; these periods may last from a few weeks to a few months. Other animal species—for instance, insects, riverine crustaceans, or schooling fish—also exhibit marked seasonal fluctuations in availability and abundance because of mating or feeding behavior; they congregate during mating season or in places where food is abundant.

Archaeologists have employed the contents of coprolites to ascertain the time of the year that a particular site was occupied. The shape, form, and size of coprolites are frequently specific to particular species or genera; consequently, it is usually possible to distinguish human coprolites from those of other animals. Some of the items found in human coprolites that indicate seasonality include the plumage of immature birds, pollen incorporated either by ingestion or inhalation, the skeletal remains of small vertebrates displaying diagnostic, age-specific characteristics, and seeds or other macrobotanical remains.

Archaeologists have also used fruits with internal seeds—for example, avocados, tomatoes, apples, or berries—and other macrobotanical remains to determine seasonality. Because the growth cycles of plants are seasonal, the presence of fruit seeds or other macrobotanical remains characteristic of a particular time of the year indicate, often to within a few weeks or a month, the season when they were consumed or used, provided that the plants were grown locally or in the same small region. For example, high concentrations of blueberry seeds—a plant that ripens in July and August—in the deposits of a site would suggest that it was used during this season, since the fruit decays rapidly.

Finally, the nature of the sediments forming the matrix of the archaeological deposits have been used as seasonal indicators. Waterborne sediments are composed of fine, rounded particles, as opposed to the angular particles characteristic of wind-blown soils. By examining the nature of the sediments in which the cultural remains occur and knowing the time of the year when these sediments are deposited in that locality, archaeologists can determine when the site was used. Seasonal precipitation can affect the relative acidity of sediments by combining with or leaching the mineral salts found in them; as a result, sediments deposited during the wet and dry seasons in a particular locality may have different pH values. By knowing how precipitation affects the acidity–alkalinity of soils in that locality, archaeologists can determine whether a site was used during the wet or dry season.

All the techniques mentioned above allow archaeologists to draw tentative conclusions concerning the time of the year when a site was used or activities took place; however, before they can make a final assessment, it is essential for them to show that the site was not occupied or that the activities did not occur at other times of the year. Archaeologists have used many of the same techniques to demonstrate a site was not used or that something did not occur during certain seasons. For example, some species of animals—bats, for instance—will not live in close proximity to humans during the breeding and birth seasons; consequently, the presence of feces from this species in a site would indicate that it was not used during the time of year corresponding to breeding and birth season of the bats.

Depending on how time and space are integrated into particular productive systems, these operating conditions can yield relatively stable and enduring configurations, or they can be quite disruptive with respect to their objective requirements (Flannery 1968).

REFERENCES

Bökönyi, S. (1972). Zoological evidence for seasonal or permanent occupation of prehistoric settlements. In Peter J. Ucko, Ruth Tringham, & G. W. Dimbleby (Eds.), *Man, settlement and urbanism* (pp. 121–126). London: Gerald Duckworth & Co.

Crabtree, Pam J. (1990). Zooarchaeology and complex societies: Some uses of faunal analysis for the study of trade, social status, and ethnicity. In Michael B. Schiffer (Ed.), *Archaeological method and theory* (Vol. 2, pp. 155–206). Tucson: University of Arizona Press.

Flannery, Kent V. (1967). The vertebrate fauna and hunting patterns. In Douglas S. Byres (Ed.), *The prehistory of the Tehuacán Valley* (Vol. 1, pp. 132–178). Austin: University of Texas Press.

Flannery, Kent V. (1968). Archeological systems theory and early Mesoamerica. In Betty J. Meggers (Ed.), *Archeology in the Americas* (pp. 67–87). Washington, DC: The Anthropological Society of Washington DC.

Heizer, Robert F. (1960). Physical analysis of habitation residues. In Robert F. Heizer & Sherburne F. Cook (Eds.), *The application of quantitative methods in archaeology*, New York: Viking Fund Publications in Anthropology. (See especially, settlement patterns, pp. 112–115.)

Mészáros, István. (1987). Customs, tradition, legality: A key problem in the dialectic of base and superstructure. In William Outthwaite & Michael Mulkay (Eds.), *Social theory and social criticism: Essays for Tom Bottomore* (pp. 53–82). Oxford: Basil Blackwell.

Monk, Gregory G. (1981). Seasonality studies. In Michael B. Schiffer (Ed.), *Advances in archaeological method and theory* (Vol. 4, pp. 177–240). New York: Academic Press.

THE DATA AND THE PROBLEM

Archaeologists examined four sites in the same region discussed in the earlier problems, so it is necessary to make reference to evidence they furnished; three of the sites were newly discovered (Figure 5–1). Archaeologists found the following information useful in attempting to determine when each site or activity area was used, what activities occurred, how the activities were organized, and who took part in them.

Site 17 This newly discovered site, 40 kilometers east of the village at Site 16, is a rock shelter located in the mountains near outcrops of turquoise and anthracite coal. Excavations of half of the refuse deposit, which covered the entire floor of the shelter as well as a small area of the hillside in front of it, yielded four scraps of paired-warp twined cotton textiles, three fragments of net bags, one basket, and 413 small chips of turquoise and anthracite coal. The excavations also produced 101 pieces of egg shell from Bird Species 3 and 4, 37 human coprolites, 3 of which contained the feathers of 1-month-old fledglings of

Bird Species 3, and 5 of which contained the jawbones of 6-month-old individuals of Fish Species 2. Seventy-five bones of Bird Species 1, representing a minimum of 14 individuals, were recovered. In addition, 752 feces identified as Mammal Species 1 were also collected.

Site 18 This newly discovered site is located on an alluvial fan at the mouth of the river. It is flooded from December to May of each year because of heavy rains. The excavations uncovered fragments of fiber mats and nets, scrapers, and three Canario projectile points that were incorporated in a single layer of windblown sediments deposited during the summer and autumn dry season. Other seasonal indicators included 183 coprolites with 1- to 2-month bones of Bird Species 2; 73 human coprolites with fledgling plumage of Bird Species 2; 37 bones of 1- to 2-month-old fledglings of Bird Species 2; 42 bones, representing nine individuals, of Bird Species 1; 17 bones of Fish Species 1; 1 skull without antlers and 13 bones of Mammal Species 4; and 1,543 individuals of Mollusk Species 1—all of which had four growth bands, the first and third of which indicate periods of maximal growth.

Site 19 This newly discovered open campsite is located in the mountains, 20 kilometers inland and east of Site 16. Excavations conducted on about 40 percent of the site yielded postholes and the remains of two huts made from branches. One domestic structure had five rocking milling stones and grinding slabs associated with it, and the other had six. The refuse deposits yielded eight scraps of paired-warp, twined cotton textiles, 19 basket fragments, and four triangular-shaped obsidian projectile points. The excavated animal and plant remains indicating seasonality are 14 bones, including one skull fragment with mature antlers, of Mammal Species 3; 42 bones, including fragments of three skulls with mature antlers, of Mammal Species 4; and 123 bones, including portions of five skulls with mature antlers of Mammal Species 5. Also found were 405 complete specimens and several hundred thousand shell fragments of Plant Species 1.

Site 16 Limited excavations in two selected portions of the village settlement yielded the following information.

Area 1 had habitation refuse deposits behind three of the eight houses with plastered stone walls. The patches formed a single continuous dump, and the excavation exposed a continuous single stratum of refuse that yielded 201 scraps of paired-warp, twined cotton textiles and domestic refuse: marine fish, deer, and bird bones; squash stems, avocado pits, lucuma shells, pacae pods, marine mollusks, the carapaces of marine and riverine crustaceans, cotton seeds, and ocas. Indicators sensitive to seasonality included 843 specimens of Plant Species 1, 8,236 seeds of Plant Species 2, 405 bones of Bird Species 1,

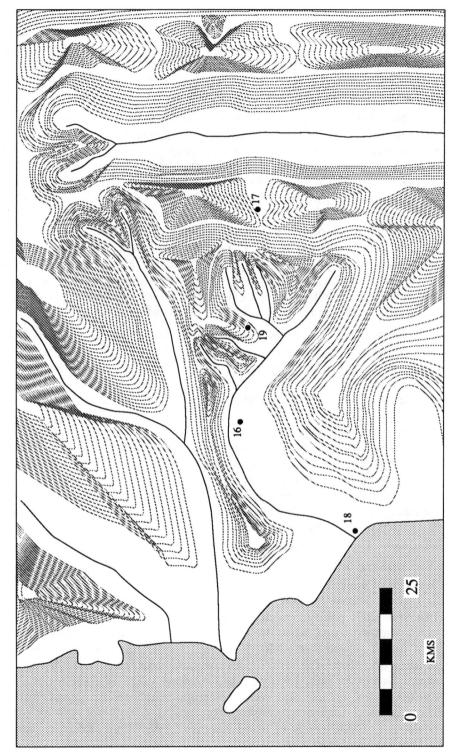

Figure 5–1

532 bones of 1-month-old Mammal Species 2, 7 skulls with mature antlers of Mammal Species 3, and 7,033 bones and 742 scales from Fish Species 1.

Area 2 consisted of six stone-lined pithouses, resembling those from Site 2, and associated refuse deposits. These were located 200 meters from the pyramid and the houses of Area 1. The refuse contained paired-warp, twined cotton textiles indicating the contemporaneity of Areas 1 and 2. The seasonal indicators in the debris included Fish Species 1, eggshells and the remains of newborn fledglings of Bird Species 3, and Plant Species 2. Eight burrows and nests of Bird Species 4 were uncovered in contexts contemporary with the refuse.

Botanists and zoologists provided the following information about the species that were recovered from the four sites excavated in the region.

Mammal Species 1 Bat intolerant of other species during its June–August breeding–birth season.

Mammal Species 2 Camelid with March–April birth season.

Mammal Species 3 Cervid that sheds its antlers in January; antlers with velvet from April to early September and mature antlers from September to early January.

Mammal Species 4 Cervid that sheds its antlers in late October; antlers with velvet from January to mid-April and mature antlers mid-April to late October.

Mammal Species 5 Cervid that sheds its antlers in April; antlers with velvet from mid-July to October and mature antlers from October to April.

Bird Species 1 Migratory species available locally in November and March.

Bird Species 2 Marine species with late May birth season.

Bird Species 3 Land species with late April to early May birth season.

Bird Species 4 A burrowing owl that is intolerant of other species during its August–October breeding–birth season.

Plant Species 1 Nut tree that ripens in September and October.

Plant Species 2 Fruit that ripens in May and June.

Mollusk Species 1 Marine mollusk with maximum growth period occurring during the fall and winter. They add maxima and minima growth bands each year.

Fish Species 1   Fish that spawns in the rivers during July and August.

Fish Species 2   The young hatch in October.

To answer the following questions, it is necessary to keep in mind the chronological relationships you established in Problems 2 and 3. When was Site 17 occupied? What happened there? What happened in the vicinity of the site? Who participated in these activities? What does this indicate about the social organization of the communities that resided in the larger region? When was Site 18 occupied? What happened there? What happened in the vicinity of the settlement? Who participated in these activities? What light does Site 18 shed on the organization of settlement and subsistence activities during the period it was used? When was Site 19 occupied? What happened at the campsite and in its environs? Who participated in these activities? What does this tell us about the social organization of work of the communities that occupied the larger region? When were the two areas of Site 16 occupied? What does this indicate about the social organization of that community?

DISCUSSION OF THE PROBLEM

The first step in determining the seasonality of occupation of a site is to establish what times of the year it was occupied and to determine whether there is any evidence indicating that it was not used during some particular time of the year. The second step is to determine what activities occurred at the site or are represented by the objects and associations found there. The third is to ascertain whether there is any evidence indicating who took part in the activities.

The human coprolites from Site 17 contain two seasonal indicators: bird feathers and fish bones. The presence of 1-month-old fledgling feathers from Bird Species 3 indicates a May to early June occupation. The bones of Fish Species 2 indicate an April occupation. The bones of Bird Species 1 suggest the site was used in March, November, or both. Finally, the feces of Mammal Species 1 suggest that the site was not occupied during the period from June to August. The evidence can be summarized in tabular form.

	Jan.	Feb.	Mar.	Apr.	May	June	July	Aug.	Sep.	Oct.	Nov.	Dec.
Bird 1			x								x	
Bird 3					x —— x							
Fish 2				x								
Mammal 1						x ——————— x						

　　　These data indicate that the site was probably occupied from March to May, given the presence of the bats. It may have been used November as well. It was not occupied from June to September. There is no evidence indicating the duration of occupation.

　　　The occupants of this seasonal campsite harvested eggs and fledglings and fished in a nearby stream, possibly with nets. The textile scraps, paired-warp, twined cotton textiles, indicate that they came from the village at Site 16 or a contemporary but still-unknown settlement. The small chips of turquoise and anthracite coal in the refuse, as well as the proximity of outcrops, suggest that their primary reason for visiting the rock shelter was to quarry these minerals, chunks of which were then carried back to the village—that is, Site 16—where they were transformed into beads and other objects by the adult women who worked at least part time as lapidaries and jewelers. There is no evidence that male residents of Site 16 worked or quarried minerals. Thus, one can infer that the rock shelter was visited for a month or so each spring and perhaps again in the fall by one or more of the female lapidaries and jewelers from Site 16 to quarry minerals that were made into useful objects at some other time or times of the year in the village.

　　　The cultural remains—especially the Canario projectile points and the absence of single-warp twined cotton textile fragments—suggest that Site 18 is contemporary with the assemblage from Stratum U in Problem 2 and with the materials from Sites 3, 6, and 15 in Problem 3. The sediments indicate that Site 18 could be used only during the summer and fall months because it was flooded during the rest of the year. The presence of fledglings of Bird Species 2 indicates a late June to late July occupation; the specimens of Mollusk Species 1, showing the last growth band as a minimal one, suggest a spring or summer occupation; and the presence of Fish Species 1 indicates use in July and August. The skull without antlers of Mammal Species 4 indicates an occupation from late October to late December. The bones of Bird Species 3 indicate that the site was used in March, November, or both; however, the fact that the site was flooded in the spring suggests strongly that the birds were taken in November. The evidence can be summarized in tabular form.

	Jan.	Feb.	Mar.	Apr.	May	June	July	Aug.	Sep.	Oct.	Nov.	Dec.
Bird 2						x——x						
Bird1			x									
Fish 1							x——x					
Mollusk 1			x———————————————x									
Mammal 1										x——x		
Sediments						x————————————x						

These data indicate that the site was used twice during the year. The earlier occupation occurred during the summer from late June at the earliest to August at the latest, judging by the presence of Bird Species 2 and Fish Species 1. The later occupation occurred in November, judging by the presence of Bird Species 1, although it could have begun as early as October because of the presence of Mammal Species 4. The sediments indicate that the fall occupation probably did not extend into December due to flooding accompanying the onset of the rainy season. The data also indicate that different food procurement strategies were practiced in the summer and fall at this site. During the summer, the occupants killed and consumed small birds and collected shellfish; during the fall, they killed cervids and migratory birds. The sediments indicate that the site could not have been occupied from December to May. The single refuse layer suggests that it was used for only 1 year. Site 18 provides evidence that groups, contemporary with or identical to those represented at Sites 3, 6, and 15 also established temporary campsites at different times of the year in places where certain seasonally available food resources became locally plentiful.

The faunal and botanical remains indicate that Site 19 was most likely occupied during the fall. The mature antlers of Mammal Species 3 indicate late September to January occupation. The three skulls with antlers of Mammal Species 4 indicate an occupation that extended from October to January. The five skulls of Mammal Species 5 with mature antlers indicate a possible occupation from October to April. The remains of Plant Species 1 suggest an occupation no earlier than September to October; however, nuts are stored easily, and the occupation could have been much later in the year. The evidence can be summarized in tabular form.

	Jan.	Feb.	Mar.	Apr.	May	June	July	Aug.	Sep.	Oct.	Nov.	Dec.
Mammal 3	x								x ————————————————			
Mammal 4	x									x ———————————		
Mammal 5	x ———————————— x									x ———————————		
Plant 1									x	x - - - - - - - - - - - -		

The data from Site 19 indicate that this seasonal campsite was probably occupied in late September and October, although it could have been occupied as late as April. It was also contemporary with the village at Site 16 and demonstrates that not all of the productive activities associated with the village community occurred in that village itself. Judging by the association of spears tipped with triangular-shaped points and adolescent burials at Site 16, the campsite was inhabited during the fall by teenage males and females who hunted three species of deer. However, the remains at the campsite indicate that their major productive activities involved harvesting nuts and grinding them with rocker milling stones before transporting the nut meal back to the village in baskets.

Site 16, Area 1, was probably occupied throughout the year. The only month that is not covered by the seasonal indicators found at the site is February. The seasonal evidence can be summarized in tabular form.

	Jan.	Feb.	Mar.	Apr.	May	June	July	Aug.	Sep.	Oct.	Nov.	Dec.
Plant 1									x ——	x ——	——	——
Plant 2					x	x						
Bird 1			x								x	
Mammal 3	x								x ——	——	——	——
Mammal 2				x ——	x							
Fish 1							x ——	x				

Site 16, Area 2, was occupied seasonally, presumably by individuals from a coastal fishing settlement. The seasonal evidence suggests the refuse was deposited between May and August.

	Jan.	Feb.	Mar.	Apr.	May.	June	July	Aug.	Sep.	Oct.	Nov.	Dec.
Plant 2					x ——	x						
Fish 1						x ——	x					
Bird 3				x ——	x							
Bird 4								x ——	——	x		

The excavations in Site 16, Areas 1 and 2, indicate that the former was used and presumably inhabited continuously throughout the year, while the latter was occupied seasonally each year for about 3 months in the late spring and early summer. Those individuals, who visited the village on a seasonal basis each year, may well have contributed labor power to the construction of the pyramid described briefly in Problem 4 and participated in the activities that occurred on its summit. This also implies that the residents of the farming and fishing settlements were enmeshed in a wider set of social relations that functioned at the level of the regional community.

The seasonally occupied campsites, apparently linked with the farming settlement, indicate that technical divisions of labor based on age and gender became evident at particular times of the year and in particular places but that the age and gender identities of the individuals who pursued these practices had changed.

The analyses conducted for this problem show how time and space condition production and the social relations of production. First, they show that production and social relations are contingent—that is, they are planned for certain seasons and places, they occur, and then they are replaced by other activities, practices, and webs of social relationships. Second, they show how people do things as socially situated agents rather than as the consequences of structures or systems. Third, they suggest that the social identities of individuals in a community are complex and that different aspects of these identities come to the fore as the human agents move from one frame to the next. Fourth, they imply that social identities cannot be portrayed as either monolithic or constituted by a single coherent symbolic system. Fifth, the inquiries provide us with a way of understanding the complexity of social identities, the formation of social groups, the organization of their traditional activities and practices, and interplay of authority and consent.

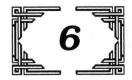

6

The Construction
and Transformation
of Regional Landscapes

A landscape is the spatial manifestation of the relations between the members of a historically specific community and their environment. It includes the sites where they live and work, the roads that link them, and the unoccupied or infrequently used places they infuse with meaning (Marquardt & Crumley 1987). The landscape created by a particular society is determined by the interplay of (1) the forces of production—that is, the raw materials appropriated, transformed, or used by its members, the tools they employ to do so, and their labor power and knowledge; (2) the relations of production—that is, who controls the productive forces as well as the production, circulation, distribution, and consumption of the useful items or goods; (3) the historically contingent structures and processes of nature created by the interaction of climate, topography, geology, and biotic communities; and (4) how the members of that society understand, interpret, assess, and assign significance and value to natural structures and processes (Levins & Lewontin 1985: 133–142, 278–285; Patterson 1993). Landscapes can be studied by the material imprint, or signature, that each society leaves on the earth's surface.

LANDSCAPE SIGNATURES

Societies with different modes of production leave different landscape signatures. This means that two societies, occupying and transforming the same part of the earth's surface at different times, may construct fundamentally different landscapes. In fact, many parts of the world today exhibit complex sequences of landscapes and landscape signatures, one superimposed on top of the other.

For example, during the first millennium B.C., particular areas along the Connecticut River Valley of western Massachusetts and Connecticut—composed of settlements, fishing sites, sacred places, and resource locations for raw materials, like nuts, quartz for tools, or wood for carving—were constituted as homelands; their communally organized occupants moved with different rhythms—daily, seasonal, annual, and irregular—on the footpaths that connected the various parts of their homeland. About A.D. 1000, these peoples adopted maize agriculture and consequently redefined their homelands and landscapes. Women began to cultivate maize in planting fields, some of which covered 20 to 40 acres, thereby assuming new roles in production and the reproduction of everyday life. Quasi-permanent villages appeared near a few planting fields, even though most of the community continued to reside in dispersed households that were linked by footpaths to each other and to the fields, hamlets, and other parts of the landscape.

After 1636, European merchants and a steadily increasing number of settler colonists intruded into the Connecticut Valley communities that were already engaged in the fur trade and whose numbers had been decimated a few years earlier by a smallpox epidemic. The fur trade flourished for a few decades, attracting men from the indigenous communities to maintain trapping lines in and beyond their traditional homelands. For the Europeans, this short-lived landscape was constituted as commodity exchange appeared on the frontier of Dutch and English settlement. By the mid-17th century, the landscape was transformed once more, as the settler-colonists displaced the native communities and seized their planting fields; the indigenous peoples, deprived of essential food resources, either died or fled to parts of the valley and their traditional homelands that the settlers considered remote or marginal. The English-speaking settlers also built palisaded villages to protect themselves from raids by the French and their allies. The dominant landscape of the valley was still shaped by commodity exchange, as the settler class shipped plant foods, dried fish, livestock, and timber to the slave-based sugar plantations of the Caribbean. This market disappeared after the War for Independence.

From the early years of the 18th century to the Revolution, the Connecticut Valley was also marked by distinctive styles of tombstones, architecture, and interior furnishing. These disappeared in the early 19th century, as the dominant landscape was again transformed. Members of the settler community built factories at the water falls near many of the old fishing sites and sold the crops they grew on the planting fields they had stolen or taken over in a regionally based capitalist economy (Russell Handsman, personal communication 1992; Merchant 1989; Paynter 1982; Thomas 1976).

The Connecticut Valley illustrates how a physical space on the earth's surface, appropriated in different ways at different moments in the past, was recast or re-created as a new or modified second nature in terms that manifest and reveal its social and cultural origins. That is, the diverse understandings and interpretations of nature are social and cultural. In the same manner, the production of a landscape—and hence the making of history itself—are "...both the *medium* and the *outcome* of social action and relationship" (Soja 1985: 94).

It is also clear that the Connecticut Valley landscapes operated at different scales (Crumley 1979). That is, they constituted regions or parts of regions that varied considerably in shape, size, extent, and duration. The two earlier ones were totalities in themselves, each broadly resembling contemporary landscapes constituted elsewhere in the river valleys of southwestern New England. These landscape changes were frequently associated with transformations occurring at the household or village level or in other cultural realms.

The landscape of the 17th and 18th centuries was different; it was located on the periphery—an increasingly specialized part—of a larger totality, whose centers of gravity were elsewhere and whose motors of development were driven by commercial activity in Boston and New York, by class-based consumer demands in England and northwestern Europe, by the demand for food and other basic necessities on Caribbean plantations, and by genocide and ethnocide. The merchants and colonists transformed the landscape they found: The indigenous peoples were ultimately killed, assimilated, or forced to move into areas that were simultaneously parts of their traditional homelands and parts of the newly emerging landscape that were perceived as marginal by the politically dominant settler class. Unlike its predecessor, the landscape, which crystallized around 1800, was situated near the center of a new totality that was driven by commodity production and the consumption needs of people residing elsewhere along the eastern seaboard and in the interior of North America in the newly formed nation-state called the United States. Several other dominant landscapes have appeared in the valley since then, including the current one, which incorporates copies or restorations of colonial buildings, infused with new meanings, and Cape Cod bungalows carefully placed in bucolic settings.

The landscape signatures inscribed on the earth's surface allow archaeologists to recover the landscapes and regions invested with meaning by ancient societies. Archaeologists examine the archaeological record in order to answer a number of questions.

First, did the members of a particular ancient community carry out the same activities at a number of contemporary archaeological sites, or were their everyday activities differentially distributed in time and space and structured by diverse temporal rhythms and socially produced understandings of space?

Second, what were the associations between the activities that occurred at particular sites and the various natural structures and processes that occurred around them? That is, which aspects of the historically contingent environment were significant to the community, and what meaning did its members assign to these features?

Third, were certain activities always carried out in the same place? In other words, did they cluster in some significant way, and how were they related to that historically constituted landscape as a whole?

Fourth, was there some sort of regular spacing or travel time between similar kinds of sites; between different kinds of used, infrequently used, and unused areas; and what accounts for both the regularities and irregularities? For instance, were adjacent farming hamlets spaced about 10 kilometers apart, whereas each was located 5 kilometers from a center as central place models might suggest? Fifth, what are the distinctive features of the linkages that exist among the various elements of the landscape constructed by a particular community? Sixth, what were the motors of development that dissolved one landscape and transformed it into a new one?

REFERENCES

Crumley, Carole L. (1979). Three locational models: An epistemological assessment for anthropology and archaeology. In Michael J. Schiffer (Ed.), *Advances in archaeological method and theory* (Vol. 2, pp. 141–173). New York: Academic Press.

Levins, Richard, & Richard Lewontin. (1985). *The dialectical biologist.* Cambridge, MA: Harvard University Press.

Marquardt, William H., & Carole L. Crumley. (1987). Theoretical issues in the analysis of spatial patterning. In Carole L. Crumley & William H. Marquardt (Eds.), *Regional dynamics: Burgundian landscapes in historical perspective* (pp. 1–18). San Diego: Academic Press.

Merchant, Carolyn. (1989). *Ecological revolutions: Nature, gender, and science in New England.* Chapel Hill & London: University of North Carolina Press.

Patterson, Thomas C. (1993). Towards a properly historical ecology. In Carole L. Crumley (Ed.), *Historical ecology.* Sante Fe: SAR Press.

Paynter, Robert. (1982). *Models of spatial inequality: Settlement patterns in historical archeology.* New York: Academic Press.

Soja, Edward. (1985). The spatiality of social life: Towards a transformative retheorisation. In Derek Gregory & John Urry (Eds.), *Social relations and spatial structures* (pp. 90–127). New York: St. Martin's Press.

Thomas, Peter A. (1976). Contrastive subsistence strategies and land use as factors for understanding Indian–White relations in New England. *Ethnohistory, 23* (2), 1–18.

THE DATA AND THE PROBLEM

Archaeologists reexamined some of the sites discussed in the earlier problems (shown in Figure 6–1), so it is necessary to refer to the evidence they provide and to the inferences you have already drawn from this information. In addition, they also conducted more extensive inquiries and excavations at sites discussed earlier and at two new sites. They also paid close attention to the chronological relationships and contemporaneity of sites—that is, which ones could be assigned to the same period of time based on the chronologically significant features of their contents.

Phase 1

So far, four sites—3, 6, 15, and 18—are known to date to this period. Extensive excavations had already been conducted at Site 15 (Problem 4) and Site 18 (Problem 5). Further analyses of data already recovered and small excavations conducted at Sites 3 and 6 yielded the following information.

Site 3   Site 3 (Problems 3 and 5) is situated 3 kilometers from the cliffs overlooking the ocean in a habitat with lush vegetation that is bathed by continual heavy fogs from June to October. The seasonal indicators include the remains of locally available grasses that ripen between July and September, mature antlers from Mammal Species 4, and antlers with velvet of Mammal Species 5. Other food remains include marine mollusks and fish from the rocky headland habitats found at the foot of the cliffs. Fragments of bottle gourds, which do not grow locally, were also plentiful in the refuse. Traces of four circular thatched houses were uncovered.

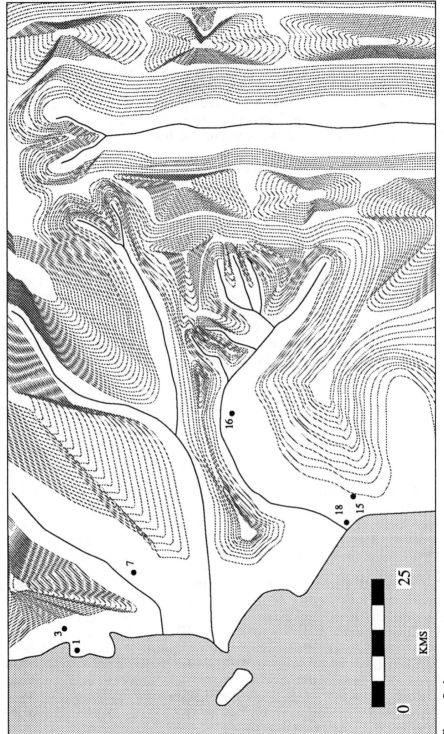

Figure 6-1

Site 6 Site 6 (Problems 3 and 5) is situated on a river terrace about 6 kilometers from the ocean and overlooks the seasonally inundated (December–May) stream. The plant and faunal indicators of seasonality recovered in the habitation refuse were Bird Species 1, eggshells of Bird Species 3, Plant Species 2, and Mammal Species 4 antlers with velvet. The food remains also included marine mollusks from both beach and rocky headland habitats, and marine fish. The refuse deposits yielded 11 thorn needles and two bone bodkins as well as considerable quantities of reeds and sedge that grow throughout the year in riverbank habitats, stone drill fragments, and bone bead fragments that broke while they were being shaped and drilled.

Seven circular thatched houses were built about 8 meters apart on the terrace overlooking the stream. Beyond the houses and the refuse deposits associated with them was a rectangular plaza, 30 by 10 meters, that was cleared of rocks and flanked by boulders. Beyond it were remains of two circular thatched houses and the postholes of a circular structure about 4 meters in diameter with a central hearth.

Site 15 Site 15 (Problem 4) is situated adjacent to a small permanent spring. It sits between the valley floor habitats and an area covered with lush fog vegetation from June to October. It is located 6 kilometers from the ocean and about 7 kilometers from the river. Further analysis of the seasonal indicators recovered at Site 15 indicate that the settlement was occupied continuously throughout the year.

Site 18 Site 18 (Problem 5) was a campsite occupied only 1 year. People gathered from July to August to hunt birds and collect riverine shellfish and later in November to hunt deer and migratory birds.

Phase 2

Three Phase 2 occupations were located in the early survey— Site 1 Lower Stratum, Site 4 Lower Stratum, and Site 7 (Problem 3). Extensive excavations were made in the lower stratum of Site 1 and at Site 7.

Site 1 Lower Stratum This settlement is situated on a hill slope overlooking marine habitats found at sandy beaches and rocky headlands. The settlement is located 150 meters from the ocean, 4.5 kilometers from the nearest fog vegetation habitat, and 12 kilometers from the nearest spring. Seasonal indicators in the habitation refuse suggest that the settlement was occupied continuously throughout the year; the food remains consisted of marine fish, especially enormous numbers of small schooling anchovies, beach and rock-dwelling mollusks, crustaceans, seals that live and breed on a rocky beach north of the village between January and March, wild fruits that ripen at different times of the year in valley bottomland habitats, and a few chili peppers and peanuts. The cultural remains in the refuse consisted of bottle gourds used as water containers, cooking vessels, and net floats; grooved stone weights; hammerstones, thorn, and shell fishhooks; large numbers of cotton net fragments; scraps of single-warp, twined cotton textiles; spindle whorls for spinning cotton thread; gourd float; bone needles; and bodkins. Excavations yielded traces of four semisubterranean, rectangular houses, measuring about 3 by 5 meters, each of which had a hearth next to the entrance; and the remains of eight stone-lined pithouses, averaging 78 by 170 centimeters, clustered around three food preparation areas.

Site 7   Site 7 is a single-component habitation settlement situated on the high terrace of a seasonally inundated stream and overlooks approximately 150 hectares of valley bottomland that is typically flooded for few weeks each year in January. It is located 17 kilometers from the mouth of the river and about 12 kilometers from the ocean. Six rectangular, wattle-and-daub houses, averaging about 3 by 5 meters, formed a line along the riverbank. Each structure had a hearth adjacent to its entrance. Refuse deposits adjacent to the houses yielded a number of seasonal indicators: Bird Species 1, eggshells of Bird Species 3, Plant Species 2, Mammal Species 4 antlers with velvet, and the carapaces of riverine crustaceans available in June and July. The plant remains consisted mainly of cotton seeds, gourd and squash rinds, some domesticated chili peppers, and peanut shells. The faunal remains consisted mainly of deer (Mammal Species 4) and marine fish and mollusks. The cultural remains in the domestic refuse consisted of scraps of single-warp twined cotton textiles, cotton net fragments, and a broken triangular-shaped spear point and chipping debris from a locally available, fine-grained quartzite, and fragments of two doughnut-shaped stone digging sticks weights.

Beyond the stream and the houses that lined it was a cleared plaza, about 50 by 20 meters, that was flanked on the long sides by low piles of boulders and stones and by a low platform mound at downstream end. The summit of the 1.5-meter high, stone-faced platform mound measured 19 by 11 meters. The residents also dug a gravity-fed irrigation canal, which diverted water 1 kilometer upstream from the settlement and watered about 30 hectares of the valley bottomlands across from the settlement.

To answer the following sets of questions, it is essential to build on the information you established in the preceding problems, and to examine the relations of each site to features of the natural environment. Do Sites 3 and 6 exhibit seasonality? What subsistence activities can be inferred from their habitation refuse deposits? What is the significance of the gourds found at Site 3? What does the evidence from Site 15 indicate about how the subsistence activities were structured by age and gender? What is the potential significance of the rectangular plaza and large circular structure at Site 6? How did the Phase 1 inhabitants of this geographical area understand, construct, and use their landscape?

Do the occupations in the lower stratum of Site 1 and at Site 7 exhibit seasonality? What subsistence activities can be inferred from their habitation refuse deposits? What is the significance of the domesticated plant remains and products found at Site 1? What is the significance of the domesticated plant remains and products found at Site 7? What is the significance of the canals at Site 7? What does the evidence from Sites 1 and 7 indicate about how the subsistence activities were structured by age and gender? What is the potential significance of the rectangular plaza and large circular structure at Site 7? How did the Phase 2 inhabitants of this geographical area understand, construct, and use their landscape?

How was the Phase 1 landscape transformed into that of Phase 2? What were the historically constituted motors of development and change?

DISCUSSION OF THE PROBLEM

The seasonal indicators from Site 3 indicate that it was occupied from late April to October. Adult and adolescent women hunted deer and harvested wild fruits and grasses, while their male counterparts walked to the ocean to fish and gather marine mollusks from the rocky headland habitats. Assuming three to five occupants per domestic structure (Problem 4), the 12 to 20 residents of the camp probably used bottle gourds as containers for water droplets that condensed on and dripped off the leaves of various bushes and trees in the fog vegetation habitat.

The seasonal indicators recovered in Site 6 suggest that it was also seasonally occupied from November to June. The adolescent and adult women hunted deer from January to April and migratory fowl in November and March and harvested the eggs of Bird Species 3 in April and May and the wild fruit of Plant Species 2 in May and June. The boys and men trekked to the ocean to fish and gather marine mollusks. The occupation of the campsite coincided with the mountain rains that flooded the small river. The camp had between 20 and 35 occupants, assuming the domestic structures were all in use at the same time. The debris resulting from craft production suggests that older men and women made mats and cordage, and some of the younger women made stone tools and bone beads. By analogy with the pyramid at Site 16 (Problem 5), the plaza and circular structure may have been the site of gatherings of people from dispersed households or other camps in May and June, when the wild fruit of Plant Species 2 ripened. Such gatherings might have created the conditions for the social reproduction of the larger community.

In the Phase 1 landscape, various terrestrial and marine habitats—beaches, rocky headlands, the river, fog vegetation zones, springs, and valley bottomlands—were objects of production, from which people appropriated goods to consume, use immediately, or transform into useful objects—like tools, mats, or beads. Groups whose settlement was located in close proximity to a number of resources tended to reside permanently in the same place, whereas their contemporaries in areas where seasonally available resources were often separated by considerable distances moved from place to place during the year. Communities apparently congregated in May and June for activities that presumably occurred at plazas and large circular structures. The division of labor, organized by age and gender, divided the world into water and terrestrial spheres—the former being the domain where boys and men toiled and the latter where girls and women worked. Older men and women made cordage, mats, and nets that were used by the workers in both symbolic spheres.

Although people resided continuously throughout the year at Site 1, they lived in different kinds of domestic structures: rectangular houses and small pithouses. This suggests that there may have been more or less permanent residents and transient residents, presumably boys and men, who came from camps in the valley bottomlands with agricultural produce and who stayed to fish for varying periods of time. If the Phase 1 division of labor structured by age and gender still prevailed, then adolescent and adult women collected water and wild plant foods and killed seals during the spring, while adolescent and adult males fished with lines and nets and dove for marine mollusks. Older men and women residing in the village spun cotton thread, made fishnets, and twined single-warp textiles.

About 20 to 30 individuals resided at Site 7 from January to at least July and possibly even August or early September, judging by the seasonal indicators and the fact that all of the cultivated plant species can be still be productively harvested that late in the growing season. Individuals from dispersed households in the vicinity may also have joined them to work in the planting field where cotton, gourds, and possibly squash were the major crops and where some chili peppers and peanuts were also grown. If the Phase 1 technical division of labor, which was structured by age and gender, still held, then the agricultural work, foraging, and hunting reflected by the contents of the refuse deposits was probably performed by adolescent and adult women, while adolescent and adult males carried agricultural produce, cotton yarn and twine, cloth and fishnets to the inhabitants of coastal fishing villages and returned with dried fish and marine mollusks; they may have also have used nets to catch riverine crustaceans in June and July. The plaza and pyramid may have been the site of gatherings of people from dispersed households or other camps during the late spring or early summer, when the wild fruit of Plant Species 2 ripened. Such gatherings might have constituted the conditions for the social reproduction of the larger community.

In Phase 2, the landscape was transformed. Valley bottomland was transformed from an object of labor, provisioned by nature, that provided immediate returns to an instrument of labor—a major means of production—that yielded returns only after a series of labor investments over an extended period of time. Some individuals in the community cultivated mainly cotton and gourds, which were used or transformed into containers, cloth, cordage, or nets. Initially, the adoption of agriculture did not significantly increase the consumption of domesticated plant foods; however, it facilitated the manufacture of stronger nets and cordage that apparently made fishing a more reliable and productive subsistence activity. This was sufficient to allow communities to pursue and diversify a marginally productive activity, like cultivation, which involved delayed use or consumption. One consequence was that plant foods and other resources of some areas— for example, fog vegetation habitats—apparently declined in importance.

The new forms of production that emerged in Phase 2 transformed the landscape. These motors of change included (1) the reorganization and increased productivity of labor processes associated with the appropriation of marine resources—men's work given the division of labor that prevailed earlier; (2) the development of new labor processes associated with agricultural production and the utilization of the terrestrial landscape—women's work given the preceding division of labor; (3) the crystallization of seasonally constituted, collective activities associated with the construction of irrigation canals (they are not built when the river is flooding), plazas, and pyramids at the inland settlements; and (5) the circulation of economically important goods between farming and fishing settlements, whose economies became increasingly differentiated through time, judging by the textured, specialized agrarian landscapes that were created in Phase 3 (Problems 4 and 5).

7

Social Divisions of Labor, Class Structures, and State Formation

The kin-organized, communal societies portrayed in the preceding problems were characterized by technical divisions of labor—that is, culturally constituted differences determined who fished, foraged, or farmed. However, since all of the adults participated in the production, exchange, distribution, and consumption of useful items, there was no regular or consistent structural difference between producers and nonproducers. While such a distinction might describe given individuals in relation to one particular productive activity, it would not adequately characterize their relation to a number of similar and different productive activities. These communities also exhibited collective control and appropriation of the objects and means of production; individuals belonged to the community by virtue of their regular participation in those activities and practices that gave meaning to their interdependence (Leacock 1982: 159).

THE SOCIAL DIVISION OF LABOR AND CLASS STRUCTURES

These communal societies lacked a social division of labor, in which a group of persons—by virtue of controlling labor power and the means of production—consistently extorted labor and/or goods from the direct producers to sustain themselves (de Ste. Croix 1981: 42–45). The absence of a social division of labor—the systematic distinction between a class of producers and a class of nonproducers—implies that there was no exploitation. However, this does not mean that status differences were nonexistent, nor does it mean that social relations were not oppressive, on occasion, nor even that wealth differentials were nonexistent. Some individuals and groups in communal societies occasionally did withdraw from direct labor and depend for periods of time on the labor of others; however, their ability to appropriate the labor and the goods of others was based on the continuing goodwill of the community, since their capacity or authority to do so reflected age, life status, or kin connections rather than force or control of the community's means of production. Such dependency was fragile, and was continually renegotiated (Clastres 1987: 189–218; Gailey 1987).

There was nothing inherent in the social relations of these kin-based communities that automatically or necessarily led to the crystallization of a social division of labor. Some descriptions of kin communities stress the fact that experience and inventiveness are pooled in such communities. When crises or tasks requiring organization and supervision appear, the members of the community select temporary leaders and persuade them to serve. Tendencies toward class formation appeared when these provisional, temporary leaders were reluctant to give up their authority—that is, when they attempted to transform it into power. Such efforts necessarily required the support of others in the community. If and when they succeeded at transforming authority into power, a class structure was born.

The men and women in this new class structure could begin to pursue their own individual and individual-class interests in the context of the continuing public institutions and practices of the community. When this occurred, the social relations of the old mode of production were simultaneously dissolved and transformed into new ones as the self-proclaimed masters began to dominate their kin and neighbors and extort their labor and/or goods. Customary authority, exercised in the context of these processes, is turned into the exploitative exercise of power.

Accounts of the transition often focus on the concentration of political power—that is, legislative, administrative, and judicial power—in as few hands as possible. They examine how authority, granted for limited periods of time by the community, was usurped. Some analyses situate the original extortion of the community and the impetus for class formation in the political realm; these analyses emphasize the potential ability of charismatic war chiefs or leaders in times of crisis to seize authority and convert their retinues and/or close kin into a ruling class supported by the labor and goods of direct producers (Jacobsen 1957).

Other analyses locate the original extortion and the precipitation of a class structure in the domain of ritual personages, the custodians of ancestors' shrines, who appropriated for their own use gifts, that were formerly consumed by the community that offered them, and who successfully added political dimensions to their ritual offices and crystallized class differences between themselves and the larger community (Southall 1988). Other studies show that there were often multiple centers of power and that there were struggles both within the emergent ruling class and between its members and the direct producers who grew the food, built the palaces, and made the objects that underwrote the leisured existence of the nonproducers (Patterson 1991).

STATE FORMATION

Relations of exploitation and domination never emerge alone, isolated from other changes in the society. The appearance of a social division of labor is rooted in social processes that involve violence, repression, and conquest. Thus, the constitution of a social class structure is also connected with the formation of a state apparatus. The various institutions, practices, and legal codes of the state represent the interests of the dominant class. The state ensures counts of bodies for taxation and conscription, collects taxes and tribute, suppresses internal dissent or deflects it outward toward other communities, selects overseers and bureaucrats, establishes stationary or moving capitals, reorganizes production to satisfy new patterns of distribution and exchange, creates gender and ethnic differences, erects distinctions between town dwellers and their rural kinfolk, constructs new landscapes, conjures up archaisms to mask the significance of the new social relations by portraying them as rooted in history, and often invents even heritage and tradition themselves.

Archaeologists concerned with civilized societies—that is, those with social divisions of labor—have identified class structures and still continue to devote a good deal of attention to their remains, especially those left by their ruling classes (Paynter & McGuire 1991). They have used diverse kinds of evidence to examine unequal distribution and its consequences: These include variations in burial practices (Menzel 1976), differences in physical stature as indicators of differential dietary practices within a society (Haviland 1967), differences in the age-specific mortality profiles of different social classes (McCarthy & Graff 1980), the possession of objects exhibiting restricted use or consumption, and differences in the style or size of residential architecture and their accessibility or seclusion.

REFERENCES

Clastres, Pierre. (1987). *Society against the state: Essays in political anthropology.* New York: Zone Books.

de Ste. Croix, Geoffrey E. M. (1981). *The class struggle in the ancient Greek world.* Ithaca: Cornell University Press.

Gailey, Christine W. (1987). *Kinship to kingship: Gender hierarchy and state formation in the Tonga Islands.* Austin: University of Texas Press.

Haviland, William A. (1967). Stature at Tikal, Guatemala: Implications for ancient Maya demography and social organization. *American Antiquity, 32*(3), 316–325.

Jacobsen, Thorkild. (1957). Early political development in Mesopotamia. *Zeitschrift für Assyriologie und voderasiatische Archaologie, 52,* pp. 91–140.

Leacock, Eleanor B. (1982). Relations of production in Band society. In Eleanor Leacock & Richard Lee (Eds.), *Politics and history in Band societies* (pp. 159–170). Cambridge: Cambridge University Press.

McCarthy, John P., & Stephen H. Graff. (1980). Differential mortality and status: Implications for archaeology. Paper presented at the annual meeting of the Society for American Archaeology, Philadelphia.

Menzel, Dorothy. (1976). *Pottery style and society in ancient Peru.* Berkeley & Los Angeles: University of California Press.

Patterson, Thomas C. (1991). *The Inca empire: The formation and disintegration of a pre-capitalist state.* New York & Oxford: Berg.

Paynter, Robert, & Randall H. McGuire. (1991). The archaeology of inequality: Material culture, domination and resistance. In Randall H. McGuire & Robert Paynter (Eds.), *The archaeology of inequality* (pp. 1–27). Oxford: Basil Blackwell.

Southall, Aidan. (1988). The segmentary state in Africa and Asia. *Comparative Studies in Society and History, 30*(1), 52–82.

THE DATA AND THE PROBLEM

The following data are from a series of contemporary archaeological sites located in the region (see Figure 7–1). Analysis of chronologically sensitive artifacts—for example, red-painted pottery, similar to that from

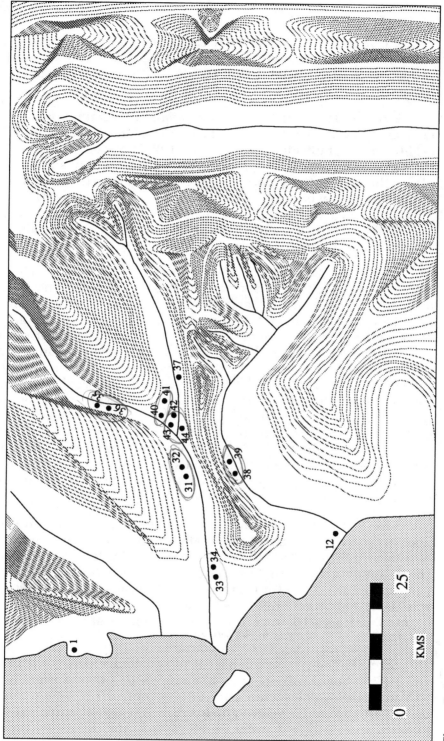

Figure 7–1

Stratum A in the excavation described in Problem 2, and decorated textiles—as well as an extensive series of absolute dates obtained from various materials associated with the sites indicate that they date from a period spanning 50 to 75 years.

Site 31. This village had 88 residential structures with covered floor areas averaging 48 square meters and an estimated population of 440 to 500 individuals. The spatial distribution of artifacts and their associations with the various residential structures indicate that all of the domestic groups engaged in agricultural production, hunting, and weaving. There was also some part-time craft specialization: Red-painted pottery vessels were manufactured by 20 households, 12 residential units produced embroidered plain-woven fabrics, and 11 made farming implements—stone digging-stick weights.

Site 32. Archaeologists excavated 800 burials at the cemetery adjacent to and contemporary with Site 31. There were 275 infants less than 2 years old and 525 juveniles, adolescents, and adults, only 10 of whom survived beyond the age of 35 years. The average stature of adult males and females were 162 ± 1.3 centimeters and 156 ± 1.2 centimeters, respectively. All the infants were buried in pottery jars placed in shallow pits. All of the juveniles, adolescents, and adults were buried in flexed position in shallow pits. Ninety-two percent of the juvenile and adult burials had associated grave goods consisting of one to three red-painted plates containing the remains of domesticated plant foods. In addition, adolescent and adult males were buried with slings and females with spinning, weaving, and sewing implements; 11 adult males were interred with hammer-stones.

Site 33. This village had 75 residential structures with covered floor areas averaging 51 square meters and an estimated population of 375 to 420 individuals. The spatial distribution of artifacts and their associations indicate that all of the domestic groups participated in agricultural production, hunting, and weaving. There was some part-time craft specialization: 21 households made red-painted pottery; 16 wove tapestries; 7 made stone digging-stick weights.

Site 34. The cemetery adjacent to and contemporary with Site 33 yielded 750 burials. There were 275 infants less than 2 years old and 475 juveniles, adolescents, and adults, only 10 of whom survived beyond the age of 35 years. The average statures of adult males and females were 162 ± 1.4 centimeters and 156 ± 1.3 centimeters,

INF B.
34.375%

AD B:
65.625%

OVER 35
1.25%

INF: 36.667%

AD:
63.3%

OVER 35   1.333%

respectively. All of the infants were buried in red-painted jars placed in shallow pits. All of the juveniles, adolescents, and adults were buried in flexed position in shallow pits. Eighty-nine percent of the flexed burials had associated grave goods consisting of one to four red-painted plates that contained the remains of domesticated plant foods. In addition, the adolescent and adult males were associated with slings and females with spinning, weaving, and sewing implements.

Site 35   The 80 residential structures with covered floor spaces averaging 49.3 square meters in the village housed an estimated 400 to 445 individuals. The spatial distribution of the artifacts and their associations indicate that all of the residential groups farmed, hunted, and wove fabrics. There was also some part-time craft specialization: 18 made red-painted pottery, 11 produced embroidered fabrics, and 8 made stone digging stick weights.

Site 36   Eight hundred burials were excavated at the cemetery adjacent to and contemporary with Site 35. There were 300 infants less than 2 years old and 500 juveniles, adolescents, and adults, only 15 of whom survived beyond the age of 35 years. The average statures of adult males and females were 162 ± 1.6 centimeters and 156 ± 2.0 centimeters, respectively. All the infants were buried in pottery jars placed in shallow pits. All of the juveniles, adolescents, and adults were buried in flexed position in shallow pits. Ninety-three percent of the flexed burials had associated grave goods consisting of one to three red-painted plates containing domesticated plant foods. In addition, adolescent and adult males were associated with slings and females with spinning, weaving, and sewing kits; 18 males were interred with kits containing stoneworking tools.

Site 37   This settlement contained 13 residential structures with covered floor areas averaging 52 square meters; a food storehouse and a warehouse where raw materials, weapons, and cloth were stored; and two workshops. Woven fabrics were produced in one workshop and stone weapons in the other. Seasonal indicators in the habitation refuse indicate that 12 domestic structures were occupied from September to December and that 1 was used throughout the year. There is no evidence that these seasonal occupants farmed, fished, or hunted while they resided at this production site; the food they consumed presumably came from the storehouse. The habitation refuse also yielded embroidered and tapestry scraps and broken and/or expended stoneworking implements.

Site 38   The 50 domestic structures with covered floor areas averaging 60 square meters housed an estimated 250 to 300 individuals. Five food storage facilities formed the southern edge of the village. There is no evidence that any of the residents engaged in food production or hunting, although some of the adolescent and adult women may have spun and wove, judging by spindle whorl fragments in the refuse deposits associated with the houses.

Site 39   One hundred two burials were recovered from the cemetery associated with Site 38. There were 22 infants less than 2 years old; the other 80 were juveniles, adolescents, and adults, 12 of whom survived more than 45 years. The average stature of the adult males and females were 168 ± 2.0 centimeters and 157 ± 1.5 centimeters, respectively. All the infants were buried in red-painted jars placed in shallow pits. The juvenile, adolescent, and adult individuals were buried in flexed position in tombs with wooden walls and cane roofs. All the flexed burials wore one to three jade necklaces and had associated grave goods consisting of pottery plates filled with domesticated plant foods. Of the adult males, 30 of the 34 had at least one additional human skull placed next to their left side; 14 of these bodiless skulls exhibited puncture wounds or depressed fractures.

Site 40   This settlement is specialized production-residential center adjacent to Sites 42 through 44. The village contained eight residential structures/workshops with covered floor areas averaging 60 square meters and an estimated population of 45 to 70 individuals. On the southern edge of the settlement, there was a storehouse containing quantities of spondylus shell, nodules of jade and turquoise, and copper, tin, gold,and silver ores. There is no evidence that the inhabitants of the village engaged in food production or hunting activities or that they produced any of the pottery they used. Seasonal indicators in the food debris indicated that the structures were inhabited continuously throughout the year; the industrial refuse associated with the eight structures indicates that they were used and inhabited by artisans: two by jeweler-lapidaries who worked with jade and turquoise, one by a metalsmith-jeweler who made alloys and gold and silver jewelry, one by potters who made a variety of archaized red-painted pottery vessels, two by woodworkers, and two by stone carvers.

Site 41   Ninety burials were excavated at this cemetery. There were 40 infants less than 2 years old, 8 were juveniles and 42 were adults, 5 of whom survived more than 35 years. The average statures of the adult males and females were 159 ± 2.0 centimeters and 156 ± 1.8 centimeters, respectively. All the infants were buried in pottery jars placed in shallow pits. All the juveniles, adolescents, and adults were buried in flexed position in pits. All the flexed burials wore one to three turquoise necklaces and had associated grave goods consisting of one to four pottery plates filled with domesticated plant foods and tool kits. The grave goods indicate that both men and women toiled as jeweler-lapidaries, metalsmiths, potters, and woodcarvers; women produced carved stone objects.

Site 42 This is a small truncated pyramid adjacent to Sites 43 and 44. The offering pits in each corner of the platform were filled with the remains of cultivated plants, marine fish, and spondylus. A storehouse adjacent to the pyramid contained small quantities of jade and turquoise jewelry, spondylus shell, and food remains. The residential structure had a covered floor space of 100 square meters and sheltered 10 to 12 individuals. There is no evidence that anything was produced at Site 42. Refuse around the dwelling yielded fragments of pottery vessels manufactured exclusively at Site 40, woven cloth, and food remains, suggesting that the house was occupied continuously throughout the year.

Twenty-four individuals were interred at the pyramid. Four adolescents—both male and female—with their hands tied behind their backs were buried under each corner of the pyramid. Each individual wore two necklaces—one made of jade and the other of turquoise. The burials coincided with the initial construction phase of the structure. The remaining eight individuals were interred in two tombs with wooden walls and thatched roofs. One contained a 50-year-old male who was 170 centimeters tall, a 25-year-old women who was 156 centimeters tall, two infants placed in archaized red-painted pottery jars; the other, more recent of the two tombs contained a 45-year-old male who was 172 centimeters tall, a 50-year-old women who was 163 centimeters tall, and two children. Both men and the woman in the more recent tomb wore jade necklaces and silver pins.

Site 43 This locality consisted of a residential structure with covered floor area of 400 square meters. The structure was divided into a kitchen area, a large public area, and four sleeping areas, one of which was half the size of the others. The sleeping areas suggest a population of 10 to 20 individuals. Refuse yielded pottery vessels manufactured exclusively at Site 40, food scraps, and cloth resembling that manufactured at Site 37. There is no evidence that anything was produced in the vicinity of this structure.

Site 44   Three large, elaborate stone burial vaults were erected next to residential structure at Site 43. Each represents a labor investment of 1 to 2 million person-days and involved the participation not only of skilled craftspeople—for example, stone-and woodworkers—but also of large numbers of unskilled laborers to acquire raw materials and bring them to the building sites. Two of the burial vaults were completed and had been used. The third was still under construction when the region was abandoned.

The earlier burial vault contained eight individuals: a 50-year-old man who was 161 centimeters tall, a 25-year-old female who was 156 centimeters tall, a second 25-year-old female who was 158 centimeters tall, a 30-year-old female who was 157 centimeters tall, three infants less than 2 years old, and a juvenile approximately 10 years old and presumably male. The adult male was interred in an elaborately carved wooden coffin with jade, turquoise, gold, silver, and spondylus inlays, which was covered by carved limestone sarcophagus. He wore a tapestry tunic and 12 necklaces—6 made of spondylus, 3 of gold, and 3 of silver. Ten gold and five silver plates filled with domesticated plant foods were placed inside the coffin. The juvenile was also interred in a carved wooden coffin. He, too, was garbed in a tapestry tunic and wore gold and silver necklaces and was associated with five silver plates containing domesticated plant foods. The three adult females were interred in flexed position; they wore tapestry garments and turquoise necklaces. The two infants were interred in archaized red-painted pottery jars. There were 200 archaized red-painted pottery plates, 20 gold plates, and 16 silver bottles in the tomb.

The more recent burial vault contained eight individuals: a 45-year-old adult male who was 170 centimeters tall, a 20-year-old female who was 158 centimeters tall, a 25-year-old female who was 159 centimeters tall, a 30-year-old female who was 166 centimeters tall, and four infants less than 2 years old. The adult male and the 30-year-old woman were interred in elaborately carved wooden coffins with jade, turquoise, gold, silver, and spondylus inlays. The coffins were covered with a carved limestone sarcophagi. He wore a tapestry tunic and 15 necklaces—9 of spondylus, 3 of gold, and 3 of silver. Ten gold, three silver, and one carved jade bowl filled with domesticated plant foods were placed inside the coffin. She wore a tapestry garment, silver pin, and spondylus and turquoise necklaces. The two younger women wore tapestry garments, turquoise necklaces, and silver pins. The four infants were interred in archaized red-painted pottery jars. There were 250 archaized pottery plates and jars, 20 gold bowls, 50 silver cups, and 3 carved jade bowls in the tomb, many of which were filled with domesticated plant foods.

This problem requires you to distinguish between the social division of labor—a division that differentiates direct producers from non-producers—and the technical division of labor that prevails within the class or among the classes of direct producers. What activities occurred at each settlement and when? How did age and gender structure the technical division of labor found at Sites 31, 33, and 35? Were the goods produced at each site consumed or used locally, or did they circulate beyond that site? What happened at Site 37? What is the evidence for part-time craft specialization, full-time craft production, and occupational specialization? Who resided at Site 38 and was interred in the cemetery at Site 39? Did the men and women experience the same levels of nutritional stress during the childhood and adolescent years? What does this suggest regarding the intersection of class and gender? Who resided at Site 40 and was interred in Site 41? What distinguished their status? How do their nutritional and health profiles compare with those of individuals residing elsewhere in the region? What happened at Site 42? What were the probable class origins of the adults buried in the two tombs? Who resided at Site 43? Who was buried in the earlier tomb at Site 44? Who was buried in the later vault at Site 44? What were the class origins of the adults? What was their class position at the time of death? Were there any significant differences in the style or size of residential structures among the various settlements? Did different groups or individuals occupy different positions in the distribution system of this society? Describe the system of unequal distribution and stratification that existed.

DISCUSSION OF THE PROBLEM

The activities carried out by the residents of the three village settlements—Sites 31, 33, and 35—were remarkably uniform. Households were units of production and consumption. Both men and women farmed. Adolescent and adult males hunted, and some made stone implements. All adolescent and adult women spun thread, wove cloth, and sewed, while a few of their number embroidered or wove tapestries. Pottery was manufactured for local consumption by about a quarter of the houses in each village; however, it is not clear whether men, women, or both engaged in its production. Pottery, farming implements, and possibly specialty fabrics circulated throughout the local village communities and were used by all of their domestic groups. The cemetery populations uncovered at Sites 32, 34, and 36 were also quite homogeneous and similar to each other. The close resemblances in terms of stature, age-specific mortality, and longevity suggest that the residents of the villages associated with them experienced similar levels of nutrition, health, and stress.

Site 37 was a production center, that was occupied for about 3 to 4 months each fall by roughly 60 men and women who came to weave and make stone weapons. Judging by the scraps of cloth and discarded stoneworking tools found in the habitation refuse, they probably came from each of the three food-producing villages, which ultimately also provided the food they consumed. Their labor power and the goods they produced during the fall months may have been tribute payments to the state and its ruling class. The one domestic structure inhabited continuously throughout the year may have been the residence of caretakers, guards, or overseers who did not engage in food production.

The evidence from Sites 38 and 39 indicate that this complex was highly specialized. Neither men nor women engaged in food production. The adult men were warriors who were ultimately interred with weapons and trophy heads; they were larger than the men in the farming communities, which indicates they had eaten better during their childhood and adolescent years than the males in the food-producing villages. This suggests they had different class origins. The women in the cemetery population had the same stature as their counterparts in the farming communities and may have come from these settlements. The fact that a greater number of individuals lived beyond 35 years suggests that they were generally healthier than the direct producers residing in the farming villages. Their status in the society was marked by the exclusive use of jade necklaces.

The inhabitants of Site 40, who were presumably the individuals interred in the cemetery at Site 41, transformed a wide variety of raw materials into finished goods: mineral ores, turquoise, jade, and spondylus. The food they ate was grown by the residents of the three farming villages; however, like the other items they used and consumed, it probably came from the storehouses at Site 37. Both men and women worked as full-time craft specialists, processing and possibly acquiring the raw materials they transformed into finished objects. The grave goods interred with the burials in Site 41 indicate that both men and women toiled as jeweler-lapidaries, metalsmiths, potters, and woodcarvers; women produced carved stone objects. While their status as full-time craft specialists was marked by turquoise necklaces, their stature and the age-specific mortality profile of the cemetery suggest that their health characteristics were not markedly different from those of the farming communities.

The construction of the pyramid at Site 42 apparently involved the sacrifice of 16 adolescents. Subsequent activities performed regularly or seasonally at each corner of the platform involved placing quantities of spondylus, plant foods, and fish in offering pits at each corner of the structure. Judging by their stature and age, the males interred in the tombs probably came from the ruling class, as did the woman in the more recent tomb. The woman placed in the earlier tomb, judging by her stature and age at death, may have come from one of the farming villages. This line of inference is also sustained by the jade necklaces and silver pins worn by the men and the more recent of the two women. The jade also links them with the warrior males interred at Site 39 and with the ruling family that resided at Site 43 and was interred at Site 44.

Site 43 is probably the palace occupied over the years by the ruling family. Nothing was produced by its inhabitants, who nevertheless consumed on a lavish scale. These items were manufactured by full-time craft specialists residing at Site 40, by women who toiled during the fall months at Site 37, and by males and females who grew food in the farming communities.

The burial vaults at Site 44 represent enormous investments of skilled and unskilled labor power. The skilled workers resided at Site 40. The unskilled workers most likely came from the farming settlements; their labor power was probably appropriated during the fall months—the same season some of their kin and neighbors toiled at Site 37. Six million person-days of labor were required to build the three burial vaults; this is an average of 80,000 person-days per year for 75 years. In other words, 800 individuals toiled 100 days a year to build the three tombs during the 75-year period.

The four adults interred in the earlier of the two burial vaults had physical statures and longevities resembling those of individuals interred in the cemeteries associated with the farming communities. The physical stature of the man and the eldest of the three women interred in the more recent vault suggest their nutrition and general health was better than those of contemporary direct producers in the farming villages; they had the same class origins, while the two shorter women may have had diets and health conditions resembling those of women in the farming villages. In other words, their class origins were in the communities of direct producers. The eldest woman may have been a principal wife with the ruling class origins, while the other women came from villages. The ruling family apparently was the only fraction of the ruling class that used gold and silver objects.

The ruling family was sustained by a group of males who generally enjoyed healthy, well-fed childhoods; these retainers resided at Site 39 and wore jade necklaces as emblems of their status. The ruling class also employed a small number of full-time craft specialists whose position was marked by turquoise necklaces. These men and women, and their children, resided at Site 40, which was located near the palace; their stature and longevity generally resembled those of the direct producers. The vast majority of the direct producers resided in the farming communities. The state appropriated their power and goods each year; the state also interfered with the productive and reproductive capacities of the village communities when it sacrificed the 16 adolescents at the pyramid. The state apparatus consisted of warriors and ritual specialists whose class origins lay in the ruling class.

State Formation: Conquest Abroad, Repression at Home

KIN-BASED AND CLASS-STRATIFIED SOCIETIES

There is an important difference between kin-based and class-stratified societies. In kin-organized communities, the continuity of the direct producers is ensured regardless of whether or not they provide the goods and labor required to support nonproducing members. In class-based societies, direct producers who withhold the goods and/or services demanded from them may be banished, evicted, executed, imprisoned, or placed in debt servitude. This distinction provides a baseline for understanding the dynamics of class formation, which necessarily begin in stratified, kin-based societies (Gailey & Patterson 1987). The processes of class and state formation create a dynamic within kin-organized societies. On the one hand, they challenge and attempt to dissolve the traditional institutions and practices of kin-based communities. On the other hand, the kin communities attempt to retain their autonomy and capacity to reproduce their traditional ways of life against the demands of the emerging class-based civil order. Diamond (1974) has called this dynamic, kin/civil conflict.

STATE FORMATION

State formation is intimately related to the crystallization of a class structure. A dominant class cannot continually appropriate goods and/or services from direct producers without incurring resistance.

While communities of direct producers are essential for the survival of nonproducing classes, producing communities that retain control over their resources and labor are inimical to the consolidation and reproduction of class relations. To survive as nonproducers, the members of the dominant class must create institutions and practices that both promote and disguise their attempts to control production. These disciplines are usually concerned with census-taking, taxation, or conscription, the burdens of which fall disproportionately on the subordinate classes. They also draw upon forms of gift-giving that are found in kin-based societies; however, they distort their content, obscuring the distinction between gifts that are given freely by their producers and tribute that is exacted from them by the state (Diamond 1951; de Ste. Croix 1984: 106–107).

The ability of states and their associated dominant classes to extract tribute—that is, labor power and/or goods—from subordinated classes and communities has varied considerably. In some instances, they were able to specify consistently what goods would be produced and what services provided and to intervene in the organization of the subsistence sector and in the reproduction of local communities. In those instances where local kin communities retained greater control over their labor potential and means of production, states were unable to specify consistently what goods and/or services were due (Gailey & Patterson 1988).

The interests of the emerging state, however, cannot be reduced simply to those of the dominant classes. While the state extracts goods and labor on behalf of the nonproducing classes, it is also concerned with the exigencies of social control and with the reproduction of class relations as a whole. As a result, the state is not a homogeneous entity. Its legal and political structures—the police, army, courts, schools, and bureaucracy— have potentially conflicting priorities. The state apparatus is subject to various pressures emanating from different factions within the dominant classes and from the direct-producing classes.

Reproducing class relations—that is, exploitation—may not entail reproducing either a particular class or a particular class structure. In those state-based societies where the ruling class is the only nonproducing class, the interests of the state and ruling class coincide. However, in state societies where there are other nonproducing classes—for example, merchants and landowners— their continued existence may challenge the interests of the ruling class. The institutions and practices of the state always operate more in the interests of the nonproducing classes than they do for those of the direct producers. To maintain or enhance the levels of exploitation and the conditions in which it occurs demands only that a class structure be perpetuated from one generation to the next (Patterson 1985).

State formation typically involves the absorption or subordination of peoples with differing traditions and levels of socioeconomic integration into an overarching tribute-taxation structure and the ideological apparatus that seeks to legitimate class relations. Not all communities are equally integrated into these structures. The juxtaposition and articulation of the range of producing communities and the forms of cooperation or resistance engendered during the process create uneven development and shifting regional class alignments. Uneven development describes the spatiality of control over production and circulation, the different ways in which communities are linked with the civil authorities. These linkages build on the social relations at hand and can enhance or exacerbate the existing differences between communities and regions.

State formation prevents local kin communities from re-creating autonomous ways of life and limits their capacity for self-determination. Civil authorities may impress conquered or incorporated peoples into the state-imposed division of labor as culturally defined groups—that is, ethnicities. In the context of state formation, peoples who attempt to retain control over their resources, products, and labor—the conditions necessary for them to continue a way of life—are threatened with annihilation, dispersal, enslavement, or other forms of state-sponsored repression, such as the imposition of state-sponsored forms of culture, like national languages.

Archaeologists have long been interested in the development of states, although they sometimes obscure the critical role played by the formation of social classes (Trigger 1974). In general, they recognize that states develop in two ways. One process of state formation occurs when members of one society conquer and subsequently exploit the members of another group. The other process of state formation occurs when organizing authorities—the "protopolitical" and "protogovernmental" institutions—of a kin-based community acquire functions that reflect the emergence of a ruling class that begins to pursue its own class interest. The two processes, which often occur simultaneously, are two sides of the same coin.

State formation, the expression of exploitation, occurs, when community-level relations of production and reproduction break down, and labor and goods are channeled in new directions. Since a society is never insulated from the effects of state formation, other changes also occur at the same time. These have included evidence for increased raiding and violent deaths, the sudden abandonment of settlements, the construction of hilltop forts, the appearance of capital cities, craft specialization, the restricted circulation of certain goods, the use of cultural elements (like art styles) to mark boundaries between communities that participated in different production-consumption networks, and commerce among peoples residing on the frontiers of the emerging state.

REFERENCES

de Ste. Croix, Geoffrey E. M. (1984). Class in Marx's conception of history, ancient and modern. *New Left Review,* no. 146, 94–111.

Diamond, Stanley. (1951). Dahomey: A Proto-state in West Africa. Ph.D. dissertation, Columbia University, Ann Arbor, MI: University Microfilms.

Diamond, Stanley. (1974). *In search of the primitive: A critique of civilization.* New Brunswick, NJ: Transaction Books.

Gailey, Christine W., & Thomas C. Patterson. (1987). Power relations and state formation. In Thomas C. Patterson & Christine W. Gailey (Eds.), *Power relations and state formation* (pp. 1–26). Washington, DC: American Anthropological Association.

Gailey, Christine W., & Thomas C. Patterson. (1988). State formation and uneven development. In Barbara Bender, John Gledhill, & Mogens Larsen (Eds.), *State and society: The emergence and development of social hierarchy and political centralization* (pp. 77–90). London: George Allen & Unwin.

Patterson, Thomas C. (1985). Exploitation and class formation in the Inca state. *Culture, 5*(1), 35–42.

Trigger, Bruce. (1974). The archaeology of government. *World Archaeology, 6*(1), 95–106.

THE DATA AND THE PROBLEM

The following data were collected from sites in the same geographical area described in the earlier problems. The archaeologists conducted extensive inquiries and excavations at several newly discovered sites (Figure 8–1). They paid close attention to the chronological relationships and contemporaneity of sites, using the stratigraphic information obtained from the upper layers of the excavation discussed in Problem 2. What chronologically significant features distinguish the pottery from Strata A-C in the excavation? Judging by the information described in Problems 1 and 2, what other activities were taking place when Strata A and B were deposited?

Phase 1

A series of radiocarbon measurements suggests that this phase had a duration of approximately 70 years.

Site 45 This was one of eight platform mounds abandoned during the this phase. Excavations indicate that the inhabitants of the area began building this stone-faced platform mound several centuries before Phase 1, and that there were periodic additions to the existing structure during the intervening years. The presence of small quantities of red-striped pottery associated with the final building phase suggests that construction stopped early in Phase 1. Seasonal indicators show that the annual, early summer activities and performances at the mound also ceased at this time. The next-to-the-last building stage, which occurred when red-striped, fiber-tempered pottery was manufactured, immediately before the beginning of Phase 1, involved about 1 million person-days of labor during a 50-year period.

Site 46 This was 1 of 18 farming hamlets abandoned during Phase 1. It was selected as a representative of this kind of settlement. Excavations revealed several building stages, judging by the superimposed house floors and the stratified sequence of pottery assemblages found in the habitation refuse. The pottery corresponded to Strata C-G in the excavated site described in Problem 2. In Phase 1, the settlement consisted of wattle-and-daub houses that were grouped into four compounds. The six to eight structures in each compound, which housed 30 to 40 individuals, were further grouped around patios. Three of the compounds had two patio groups; one had three patios.

Seasonal indicators in the earliest layers containing Phase 1 habitation refuse show that the settlement was occupied continuously throughout the year; the later layers with Phase 1 pottery and refuse exhibit seasonality showing mainly late spring, summer, and early fall occupations.

Grave goods found in tombs associated with the houses of each patio group indicate that there may have been small wealth differentials among the various residential groups in the same compounds. Figurines placed in the wall of the tombs and found in the habitation refuse associated with each domestic structure, patio, and compound indicate that they were involved in a series of practices—some carried out at the household level, some at the patio level, some at the compound level, and some at the level of the hamlet. The construction of the platform mound at Site 45 indicates that some activities had previously been organized at a regional level.

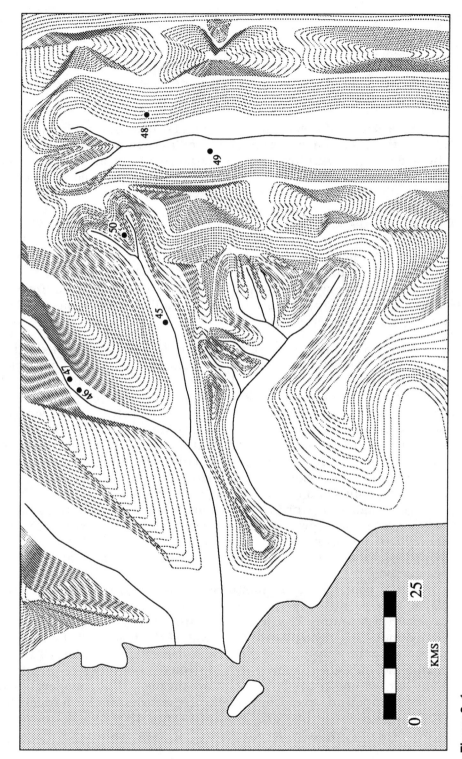

Figure 8–1

The tombs of 28 of the 32 adult males and 18 of the 21 adult females contained stone-headed maces, slings, and/or spear throwers. Three men and two women had been decapitated, and five exhibited depressed skulls and puncture wounds. Fifteen men and eleven women were interred with additional human heads; these trophy heads frequently exhibited either depressed skull fractures and/or puncture wounds. Three adult women were interred with whole spondylus shells and jade amulets. Nine men and women were also interred with pottery vessels that had been manufactured 5 to 8 centuries earlier in the area. Judging by chipping debris in the household refuse deposits, mace heads and stone projectile points were manufactured by at least one household in each patio group and by every patio group in each of the four compounds.

Site 47 A survey located 23 palisaded hilltop forts dating to this period in area; 12 are located within a kilometer of one of the farming hamlets discovered in the survey. Site 47 was selected for further inquiries and excavation. It was built and occupied exclusively during Phase 1. The construction of the two concentric stone palisades enclosing 30 domestic structures and 4 storehouses situated on a hilltop that rose 500 meters above the valley bottomlands involved at least 1.4 million person-days of labor; the size and number of houses suggest that the fortress was inhabited by about 100 to 150 individuals; seasonal indicators in the refuse suggests they occupied the site mainly after the fall harvests until planting time in the spring; chipping debris in the refuse indicates that mace heads and dart points were also manufactured. Caches of sling stones and weapons indicate that they defended themselves with stone-headed maces, slings, and darts launched with spear throwers. Some of dart points found in one cache resembled projectile points that were made and used 300 to 1,500 years earlier in the area.

Phase 2

Radiocarbon measurements indicate that this phase has a time span of about 100 years.

Site 48 This single-phase settlement was situated on the top and upper slopes of an isolated mountain mass that rises 400 meters above the valley floor. The location gave its 1,000 or so residents an excellent view of the valley floor; however, the lack of springs and arable land meant that at least some of them devoted considerable amounts of time and energy carrying food and water up the slopes. The dominant architectural feature was a 200- by 300-meter plaza that covered the summit and central ridge. The plaza was enclosed by a stone wall, 14 burial vaults with stone-lined tombs, a small pyramid faced with carved stone slabs, 20 stone-walled residential structures, each covering about 100 square meters, and a workshop-arsenal where stone mace heads, spear throwers, and darts tipped with stone points were manufactured. The construction of the whole plaza complex required about 2.8 million person-days of labor—that is, 40,000 person-days per year. Each tomb on the plaza contained the remains of an adult male. The grave goods included significant numbers of pottery vessels, fabrics, and jewelry that had been removed from earlier tombs in the area.

Site 49   Four farming villages were located on the valley floor. The three at Sites 31, 33, and 35 were buried by the later Phase 3 occupation described in Problem 7. Site 49, which had a single-phase occupation, was selected for further study. Survey revealed that the village had 72, spatially distinct, stone-walled domestic structures with covered floor areas averaging about 50 square meters. The houses were more substantial than those of the preceding phase and involved greater labor investments. The population probably numbered about 360 individuals, assuming five residents per house. Each household engaged in agricultural production, hunting, and weaving. There was also some part-time craft specialization: Women in 12 households made pottery with circumferential red-painted bands, the men in 10 houses made agricultural implements, and women in 6 households embroidered cloth. The pottery, which had a distinctive grit temper, and presumably the other goods circulated largely within the village itself. Broken storage vessels with standardized sizes were found in the habitation refuse; large quantities of these vessels were used at Site 48, although, given the absence of water, they were probably not manufactured there. Seasonal indicators in the refuse indicate that the village was occupied continuously throughout the year.

Limited excavations in a cemetery adjacent to the village yielded 25 graves: 15 adolescent and adult males were buried with slings, spears, and pottery vessels collected from earlier tombs; 6 adult men had jade necklaces. Ten adolescent and adult females were interred with spinning, weaving, and sewing implements and with locally produced plates containing domesticated plants.

Site 50   This one-phase, fortified settlement was located at the head of the valley overlooking the bottomlands of a broad intermontane basin. There is no arable land in close proximity to the settlement, which suggests that the food consumed here was grown elsewhere and transported to the settlement. Three concentric palisades enclosed 15 stone-walled residential structures with covered floor areas averaging 100 square meters, 10 storehouses containing fragments of large standardized storage vessels resembling those used at Site 48, 8 food-preparation areas, a workshop-arsenal, and a small pyramid faced with carved stone slabs. The size of the residential structures suggests a permanent population of about 150. Seasonal indicators suggest that settlement was occupied continuously throughout the year; the habitation refuse suggests they consumed large quantities of cultivated plant foods, deer, and llamas. Broken dart points and mace heads were plentiful on the surface and in the refuse deposits. Site 50 was probably a frontier garrison whose subsistence needs were satisfied by labor and goods extracted in the core area of the polity around Site 48.

What activities are represented by the three Phase 1 that were excavated? What were the real units of production and consumption in early Phase 1 society in the farming hamlets? How did they operate in the contemporary fortified hilltop settlements? How had the relations of reproduction operated before and during the early part of Phase 1? What is the evidence for seasonality? What inferences can you draw from the adult males and females buried adjacent to the houses in Site 46? Who produced weapons, and who used them? Where and when were they manufactured? How do you account for evidence indicating that the inhabitants of the farming hamlets collected earlier objects?

What activities are represented at the Phase 2 settlements? What were the real units of production and consumption at Site 49? How were they different from the farming hamlets and from the hilltop settlements of Phase 1? How was the technical division of labor in the farming settlement structured by age and gender? Who produced weapons, and who used them? Where and when were weapons used? Who resided at the Site 50? Who had access to pottery vessels and other objects plundered from earlier tombs? How were gender categories redefined during Phase 2? What is the class structure?

DISCUSSION OF THE PROBLEM

At the excavation discussed in Problem 2, the red-striped pottery in Stratum C was fiber-tempered. The red-striped pottery in Stratum B lacked fiber-temper, and the pottery in Stratum A had red-painted surfaces. This information provides the basis for distinguishing three phases: Phase 1, which is contemporary with Stratum C; Phase 2, which is contemporary with Stratum B; and Phase 3, which is contemporary with Stratum A. You examined the most recent phase in Problem 7. Old objects were collected and placed in tombs in Phase 2, and archaisms were manufactured in Phase 3.

Briefly, the archaeological evidence indicates that the construction of platform mounds ceased during the early part of Phase 1. The labor required to build the last addition to the mound at Site 45 required an average of 20,000 person-days per year—for example, 200 individuals working 100 days a year. The labor required clearly surpassed what one farming hamlet could produce; this implies that individuals from several hamlets came together each year to add to and refurbish the mound and to participate in the activities that occurred there during the early summer after planting and before the autumn harvests. Such activities functioned as community-level relations of production and reproduction.

The community-level social relations were disrupted (1) when the residents of various farming hamlets stopped building them and taking part in the activities that occurred at them, (2) when raiding disrupted everyday life in the villages, and (3) when their labor power was turned toward raiding or defense during the late fall and winter months, the manufacture of weapons throughout the year, the construction of palisaded hilltop settlements. The palisades at Site 47 required 1.4 million person-days of labor to house a population of 150, assuming 5 residents per house. This suggests a labor investment of 20,000 person-days per year over the 50-year span of Phase 1—that is, 100 individuals working 200 days per year. The labor requirements for building hilltop fortresses and retreats surpassed the labor required for pyramid construction; however, it was still raised at the level of the community, but the community itself may well have been defined in ways that emphasized the linkages between two or three hamlets rather than all of the hamlets in the area. The labor required to erect fortified hilltop sites exceeded the capabilities of a single compound and might have stretched those of an individual hamlet beyond the breaking point.

The real units of production and consumption in the Phase 1 hamlets were individual households, patio groups, and compounds. Through the early years of Phase 1, these units engaged in subsistence activities and participated in activities at one of the pyramid complexes that ensured the social reproduction of a wider community; these activities took place in the early summer. Raiding began to interfere increasingly with customary activities and practices. The injuries exhibited by the skeletal remains and the grave goods suggest that both men and women participated in raiding and the production of weapons. The increased frequency of items removed from early tombs suggests that at least some residents of Site 46 were grave-robbers, who were seeking, among other things, ancient implements that could be used as weapons. These supplemented the weapons produced by their kin and neighbors.

The organization and composition of the production and consumption units that prevailed during the summer when people resided on valley bottomlands to farm were apparently transformed during the late fall and winter, as their members moved to fortified retreats to protect themselves from raids and/or to attack neighboring groups. It is difficult to recognize either the patio or compound levels of organization in the hilltop forts.

Significant changes in settlement patterns marked the beginning of Phase 2. The farming hamlets and the fortified hilltop villages were abandoned and replaced by a hilltop capital city at Site 48, four large farming villages that concentrated the rural population, and a frontier garrison at Site 50.

The rural population was concentrated in the farming villages; however, the real units of production were apparently households rather than patio groups or compounds, since no evidence of patio groups or compounds persisted into this phase. This means that tribute in labor and/or goods was appropriated from the residents of households rather than from the village or the wider community. From the state's view, each household could be taxed. The concentration of houses into the village made it easier to oversee their residents. The more durable construction of the houses may have made their residents more reluctant to move. Part-time craft specialists continued to produce goods that circulated throughout each of the farming villages, like Site 49. For example, some young girls and women made pottery and embroidered cloth, and some boys and men made stone agricultural implements.

What is most apparent from the tombs at Sites 48 and 49 is that only males were warriors during Phase 2. Weapons and objects removed from earlier cemeteries are found only in their tombs. This contrasts markedly with the conditions that prevailed in the preceding phase, when both men and women had weapons and access to items removed from earlier graves. Furthermore, men buried and presumably residing at Site 48 had access to considerably larger quantities and varieties of goods from the earlier tombs than their rural neighbors living on the valley floor. Thus, a class structure, differentiating the inhabitants of the plaza at Site 48 from those of the farming villages, appeared at roughly the same time that evidence for cross-class, gendered activities made their appearance. Men of both classes were engaged as warriors, though men of the dominant class had access to a greater range of looted goods. Women's activities were more limited than they had been in the preceding phase, and the women who resided in the farming villages had little or no access to goods removed from the looted tombs.

Site 50 was a frontier garrison occupied throughout the year by males, presumably from Site 48 and the farming settlements in the valley. It was provisioned by the farming communities with weapons and food that was collected, stored, and moved in pottery vessels, whose sizes met the specifications of the emergent state. The existence of a fully provisioned garrison in an area where farming was not possible, suggests that raiding had become a year-round activity rather than one that occurred in the late fall and winter months.

The most invisible groups in the archaeological record recovered from Phase 2 are upper-class women, and the producers of specialized goods, like the pottery storage jars made to state specifications. While the agricultural produce and some labor service was exacted from the residents of the farming communities, it is not clear what was appropriated from the frontier communities or how the looting was organized.

Frontier Societies: State Formation and Uneven Development

STATE FORMATION

State formation is the metamorphosis of the kin-based community; it deforms and splits the community into a group that extracts tribute and subordinates the peasantry and village communities from whom labor and goods are seized. At the same time, kin communities on the margins may also be encapsulated but not fully integrated into the tributary relations and webs of dominance and dependence created by the state. Nevertheless, these frontier societies are transformed in the process, and, as Fried (1975: 98) observed, tribes are precipitated along the periphery of the emerging state. In other words, state formation creates border peoples, whose diverse property, production, and distribution relations are transformed as a result of their proximity to, domination by, and resistance to the state-based society.

UNEVEN DEVELOPMENT

There is nothing automatic or mechanical about the process of encapsulation and incorporation that occurs on the margins of states. Communities confronted with an expanding state have resisted the process of encapsulation, successfully in some instances and unsuccessfully in others. State frontiers are porous, fringe areas across which people, goods, and ideas move back and forth between the more pacified border groups and the less assimilated ones. Thus, state formation is the dialectical linkage of societies with various forms of communal and tribute-based modes of production in historically contingent circumstances that involve domination by the one associated with political rule (Gailey & Patterson 1988).

State formation produces mosaics of different kinds of societies, each characterized by distinctive political-economic, social, and cultural structures. The various kinds of kin- and class-based societies that emerge in the process manifest different forms of communal and tributary modes of production. The uneven development results from their articulation within a dominant state and political economy (Amin 1976). The form of tribute extraction determines or shapes the structures of social, political, and economic relations that develop both within the encapsulated societies and between them and the state (Thapar 1981: 410-412). These hierarchical or class structures—both those internal to a given society as well as the ones external to it—cross, merge, and interlock in various and potentially very complex combinations. They provide people with certain opportunities for making their own history and simultaneously place constraints on their actions. The forms of social reproduction and resistance to them will be embedded in a range of contradictory cultural, political, economic, and social relations and practices.

The form of tribute extraction alters the structures of social and political-economic relations that existed within formerly autonomous kin-based communities or states on their peripheries. It also shapes the relations between encapsulated kin communities and the dominant classes. Tribute extraction promotes the development of different, opposed spheres of production. Production for tribute and exchange in the encapsulated communities on the margins of states are juxtaposed and opposed to subsistence production. While these antagonistic state-oriented and kin-oriented spheres of production are politically integrated by the state, significant regional differences may emerge, depending on how the priorities of production and reproduction are reorganized among the conquered peoples, subject populations, and encapsulated communities.

In some instances, the state and its associated classes are able to extract tribute consistently and to specify what goods will be produced as tribute and what services will be provided. These strong tributary states may also be able to intervene directly in the organization of the subsistence sector and the reproduction of local communities. In other instances, tribute-based states are unable to determine in a consistent manner what labor or products will be extracted from subject populations. These weak tributary states do not have the power to intervene effectively in subsistence pursuits or local reproduction. In other words, the kin communities are effective in retaining greater control over their lands and labor potential and, therefore, can offer greater resistance to the incursion of state agents and processes (Gailey & Patterson 1988).

For the communities being encapsulated, states appear in different guises at various stages in the process. During the initial stage of contact, the state's presence may be confined to isolated garrisons and its contact with the local communities may occur at fixed places. While the state poses a threat, the communities retain use rights over their means of production and control over their labor and products. However, if the state's presence becomes more invasive, authority within the community may come to reside more firmly in the hands of members, chieftains, who are able to appropriate increased control over the movement of goods created outside the subsistence sector through activities associated with raiding and trade and through their enhanced ability to create and cement alliances with other peoples. Their real control over exchange rests more on control over their subjects than on the domination of any merchant group.

Long-distance trade relations frequently develop between the societies of the state-based center and the frontier peoples constituted along the periphery. This commerce is often mediated by money, which acts as lubricant, a universal exchange value that facilitates the process. However, it may also involve the appearance of merchant capital, which presupposes that some goods were commodities—that is, they were produced for sale rather than direct consumption; in these instances, the value of the commodities is realized by purchasing them cheaply and then selling them for larger amounts of money (Patterson 1988).

Merchant capital is attached or grafted onto and articulated with existing structures of social relations that are determined independently of it. In societies characterized by low levels of commodity production, merchants have often been viewed as parasitic intermediaries who inserted themselves between buyers and sellers, pariahs who monopolized the carrying trade and exploited both sides. By virtue of organizing and dominating long-distance trade, they existed in the interstices between the state, the village communities, the craftsworkers, and the entrepreneurs. At times, long-distance traders were socially differentiated, constituting a people-class whose occupation represented the actualization of a monetary economy (Léon 1970).

Merchant capital regulates the exchange of products between independent societies. It links them, providing each with the commodities of the others. Since it is confined to the sphere of circulation, merchant capital does not control the production processes of those societies but rather preserves them as the preconditions of its existence. However, it transforms the goods of producers, who remain separate from the circulation process, into commodities. It facilitates the transfer of a portion of the labor and goods produced, extracted, and centralized in one society to the members of another. It assigns particular functions to the autonomous and encapsulated societies of the periphery. They produce the luxury consumer goods that are brought to the metropolitan societies through exchange, plunder, or production that is especially organized for this purpose. Changes in the politics of either the metropolitan or peripheral societies or in the political relations that existed among them necessarily change the kinds of commercial relations that emerged as an integral element of the same developmental processes.

REFERENCES

Amin, Samir. (1976). *Uneven development: An essay on the social formations of peripheral capitalism.* New York & London: Monthly Review Press.

Fried, Morton. (1975). *The notion of the tribe.* Menlo Park: Benjamin Cummings.

Gailey, Christine W., & Thomas C. Patterson. (1988). State formation and uneven development. In Barbara Bender, John Gledhill, & Mogens Larsen (Eds.), *State and society: The emergence and development of social hierarchy and political centralization* (pp. 77–90). London: George Allen & Unwin.

Léon, Abram. (1970). *The Jewish question: A Marxist interpretation.* New York: Pathfinder Press.

Patterson, Thomas C. (1988). Merchant capital and the formation of the Inca state. *Dialectical Anthropology, 12*(2), 217–227.

Thapar, Romila. (1984). The state as empire. In Henri J. M. Claessen & Peter Skalník (Eds.), *The study of the state* (pp. 409–426). Paris: Mouton.

THE DATA AND THE PROBLEM

The following data were gathered in the same geographical area discussed in earlier problems, in the upper portion of the intermontane basin mentioned in Problem 8, and in two distant localities: (1) a remote mountainous area known as Old Turquoise that is located 400 kilometers north of the basin; mineral deposits containing turquoise outcrop or occur near the surface; and (2) a sandy beach, 1500 kilometers north of the area, that is washed by warm tropical waters and is adjacent to extensive beds of spondylus mollusks; it is the closest known source of this raw material. Archaeologists completed a 100 percent survey of the intermontane basin and located more than 900 sites. Figure 9–1 shows the sites mentioned in this problem.

Chemical and neutron activation analyses of the turquoise objects found at Sites 40, 41, 42, and 44 (Problem 7) indicate they came from two different sources. The objects found at Sites 40 and 41 came from local sources found near Site 17 (Problem 5). The turquoise objects found at Sites 42 and 44 have the same signatures as samples from the Old Turquoise region, which suggests the raw material came from that locality.

The red-striped pottery found at the sites described below bears a generic resemblance to the pottery found in Stratas B and C (Problem 2); however, there were also subtle differences: The highland potters used different pigments so the reds were darker and the whites were more yellowish in hue than those employed by the contemporaries on the coast; there were also subtle differences in vessel shape and design between the two localities.

A series of radiocarbon measurements indicate that this phase had a duration of about 100 years and that it was earlier than and contemporary with Phase 1 described in Problem 8.

Site 51   This was 1 of 18 dispersed hamlets, dating to this period, that archaeologists located on the heavily farmed bottomlands of the basin near springs and/or small streams; given the contemporary and historic landscape signatures, these sites are probably underrepresented in the survey. Excavations revealed the remains of six rectangular, wattle-and-daub houses with covered floor areas of about 50 square meters. Seasonal indicators in the refuse show that the hamlet was occupied continuously throughout the year; however, the most intensive occupation occurred from the fall to late spring. Production debris shows that all of the domestic groups farmed, raised guinea pigs, and spun and wove woolen cloth; five kept llama herds in the hamlet from the fall to the late spring; and at least three made their own pottery during the dry months from late spring to early fall.

One adult male and one adult female were buried next to one domestic structure. Each was interred with a guinea pig and a basin style, red-striped pottery vessel filled with peanuts and chili peppers.

Site 52   This was 1 of 23 sites, dating this period, that were found in the high grasslands ringing the intermontane basin. It was situated near a small spring. It consisted of two rectangular, semisubterranean, stone-walled houses with floor areas of about 25 square meters and a circular enclosure that was filled with llama dung. Seasonal indicators in the habitation refuse adjacent to the houses indicate that they were occupied intermittently and exclusively during the late fall and winter

KMS

0   25

Figure 9–1

months. During the birth season in late January and February, the inhabitants consumed fetal and neonatal llamas that apparently did not survive beyond the first month.

Two individuals were buried next to one of the houses. One, an adolescent female, was interred next to one of the houses with two red-striped pottery vessels—one made in the basin and the other on the coast. Six of her permanent front teeth had been extracted several years earlier. The other was an 18-year-old male interred with a basin-style red-striped pottery plate.

Phase B

Radiocarbon measurements from five of the six hilltop forts and from Sites 54 and 55 indicate that this unit had a duration of 80 years and is fully contemporary with Phase 2 (Problem 8). The beginning of Phase B is marked by the abandonment of the dispersed valley bottom farmsteads and hamlets, by the construction of six palisaded forts on the hilltops and ridges that fringe the edges of the basin, and by complete replacement of red-painted pottery by distinctive blue-painted vessels that were manufactured and used exclusively in the basin.

Site 53 This hilltop, palisaded village was selected for more intensive study and excavation. It closely resembled the other five in terms of layout, the number of structures, and probably the number of residents. It was the one located closest to the fortified garrison at Site 50 (Problem 8). Its three concentric stone walls rising to heights of 7 meters surround 70 house platforms bearing traces of wattle-and-daub domestic structures, a central plaza enclosed by 10 barracks, two workshops where stone dart points and mace heads were manufactured, and a large food storage facility. About 2 million person-days of labor were required to build the palisades. Seasonal indicators in the habitation refuse show that the fortress was inhabited continuously throughout the year, and that they relied largely on agricultural produce, guinea pigs, and deer for food. The house platforms suggest that the permanent population was about 350 individuals; another 500 individuals were housed intermittently in the 10 barracks.

Limited excavations in the large cemetery located at the foot of the hill near arable land yielded 14 burials. Seven were adult females interred with slings; agricultural implements; spinning, weaving, and sewing implements; and balls of woolen yarn. The others were adolescent and adult males buried with spear throwers and slings, agricultural implements, and tool kits for making for making dart points or ground stone mace heads. All of the burials were interred with the distinctively shaped, blue-painted pottery plates that were used throughout the intermontane basin and manufactured at one of the other contemporary hilltop fortresses. Eight of the skeletons had suffered broken arms and ribs; two had depressed skull fractures that were probably fatal; and one woman had a dart point embedded in her rib cage.

Another significant work project involved the construction of a dam across a small stream that flowed out of the mountains. The water trapped in the reservoir was used to irrigate fields and terraces located on the hill slopes immediately below the fortified settlement. The construction activities associated with the construction of the dam and reservoir involved a minimum of 150,000 person-days of labor, which was significantly beyond the capabilities of the inhabitants of the settlement. Given annual rains and flooding, the dam had to have been built during a single 8-month period. This suggests a labor force of about 625 individuals working continuously for 8 months.

Site 54   This site is located approximately 4 kilometers from the garrison at Site 50 (Problem 8) and 20 kilometers from Site 53. It consisted of three houses, two of which were occupied seasonally during the late spring. The habitation refuse associated with one house yielded small quantities of the Phase 2 archaized red-painted pottery vessels manufactured and used in the coastal valley; refuse associated with the other domestic structure yielded the distinctive Phase B blue-painted pottery of the intermontane basin. The third stone-walled house had a covered floor area 70 square meters and was apparently occupied continuously throughout the year; caches of spondylus shell and turquoise from the Old Turquoise region were found underneath the house floor. Its residents tilled a small field adjacent to the ruins, spun and wove woolen cloth, made circular spondylus beads from complete mollusk shells, and maintained a llama corral adjacent to their homestead. The domestic refuse associated with the house indicates that its residents used some red-painted pottery from the coastal valley, some blue-painted vessels from the intermontane basin, and an intrusive exotic variety, decorated with specular hematite that has no local antecedents. Cooking pots found in the habitation debris came in two sizes: one size in which about 10 servings could be prepared and another that could accommodate 50 servings.

Two individuals were buried next to the third residential structure. One was a 35-year-old adult male who lacked six front teeth. The other was a 30-year-old woman who also lacked six front teeth; both had extensive facial tattoos. Strings of spondylus beads and a single specular hematite bowl were placed in each tomb.

Old Turquoise Region

This region contains a number of turquoise-bearing veins that outcrop or occur near the surface. Prior to Phase B, the area was sparsely inhabited by small groups of llama herders who moved throughout the year from one small seasonal camp to another. Radiocarbon measurements indicate that about the time Phase 2 and Phase B developed to the south, the landscape and settlement patterns of the Old Turquoise region changed. Land was transformed from pasture to a combination of pasture and mining; a nucleated settlement appeared suddenly, as some of the former residents began to reside in the same place throughout the year and to engage in mining. Excavations were conducted at 2 of the 14 houses at this settlement. The residents of the first house—a 5-meter-square stone structure—kept a llama herd and engaged in turquoise mining, judging by the associated habitation refuse. The second structure—a stone-walled building that covered 71 square meters—yielded small caches of drilled spondylus beads and turquoise obtained from the local deposits. An adult woman missing six front teeth was buried next to the house; she was interred with a string of spondylus beads and a specular hematite bowl.

The Sandy Beach Locality

Spondylus is a warm tropical water mollusk that resides in a sandy ocean bottom habitat found at depths of 30 to 50 meters. Radiocarbon measurements indicate that there was a fishing community thrived at this waterfront location during the period when Phase 2 and Phase B pottery were manufactured to the south and when vessels decorated with specular hematite were found at scattered localities throughout the larger area. Specular hematite pottery, like that found at Site 54, occurred in significant quantities next to a compound containing four rectangular wattle-and-daub houses near the southern edge of the settlement. Seasonal indicators show that the compound was occupied continuously throughout the year; domestic and industrial debris shows that its residents farmed, had a small llama corral, spun and wove cotton, fished, and made spondylus shell beads; however, there is no evidence that they actually dove for spondylus mollusks. Three adults—two men and a woman—were buried in the compound. All of them had tattooed faces and lacked six front teeth; all were interred with a string of spondylus beads and a specular hematite bowl. Five contemporary burials in other parts of the settlement yielded three adult males and two adult females, whose skulls had been molded into a wedge shape during infancy and early childhood; they were interred with diving weights, ropes, baskets, shell fishhooks, and locally made pottery vessels.

How do Sites 51 and 52 inform us about the mode of production and social organization that shaped everyday life in the intermontane basin during Phase A? How are these patterns similar to and different from those that were appearing in the valley during Phase 1 (Problem 8)?

What does Site 53 tell us about how everyday life was transformed in the intermontane basin during Phase B? How was the kin-organized mode of production transformed? What is the significance of the construction projects at Site 53? How were the traditional technical divisions of labor redefined? How was the landscape reconfigured? What do the burials imply? What is the significance of Site 54? What does it suggest about the patterns of everyday life at that locality? Given the evidence from Old Turquoise and the sandy beach regions to the north, what do the burials at Site 54 suggest?

What information do the chemical and neutron activation analyses of the turquoise objects provide regarding the class and gender relations described in Problem 7? What is the significance of the evidence related to turquoise discussed in this problem?

DISCUSSION OF THE PROBLEM

Sites 51 and 52 suggest that the major means of production were kinds used for farming and pasture and llama herds. The members of the community resided in dispersed farmsteads and hamlets on the valley bottomlands. Individual households seem to have been the real units of production and consumption, although some items—for example, pottery and perhaps wool—circulated from one house to another. Site 52 indicates that, from late autumn to the spring, adolescent males and females herded llamas in the high grasslands and subsisted partly on animals that died during or shortly after birth. There is no evidence indicating that the highland community was other than kin-organized during this period, nor is there any indication of institutions and practices that underwrote social reproduction.

The similarities of the pottery styles used in the coastal valley and the intermontane basin indicate that there was communication between the two communities. The pottery vessels associated with the young woman interred at Site 52 in the high winter pasture indicate that exchange also occurred at this time; however, the nature of the exchange relations between the two groups is not clear.

During Phase A, the community in the intermontane basin seems to have been quite insulated from the events that were taking place in the coastal valley. There is no evidence for raiding, the reconfiguration of landscapes, or the transformation of social relations in the highland community.

The human landscape of the intermontane basin was transformed during Phase B, presumably by the presence and threat posed by the year-round garrison stationed at Site 50. The dispersed farming hamlets on the bottomlands of the basin were abandoned, as their residents congregated in newly built hilltop fortresses. The construction of the palisades at Site 53 required a labor of 800 persons working continuously for nearly 7 years; the labor demands for the palisades and for the dam—625 persons working steadily over an 8-month period—exceeded the capacities of the residents of the settlement. It indicates that labor power for the completion of these tasks was appropriated from other hilltop settlements in the basin. The barracks near the central factory and the workshop where weapons were manufactured suggest that individuals from other settlements resided at Site 53 during periods of crisis, and that the dam may have been erected to increase the amount of arable land in the immediate vicinity of the fortress. This land was used to provide agricultural produce in sufficient quantities to sustain workers and warriors who were drawn from other parts of the basin during periods of unrest; they provided a buffer against the threat of marauders from the garrison, who raided to steal or destroy crops and/or to kidnap individuals for labor service.

The earlier technical division of labor based on household or hamlet production was transformed. A remarkably uniform, blue-painted pottery was manufactured at a single site and distributed throughout the basin; herding and the production of llama wool were taken over by other residents of other settlements; defense and irrigation agriculture became the domain of Site 53. The new division of labor was still based to some extent on age and gender distinction: Men farmed and women wove at Site 53. However, gender distinctions blurred with regard to other activities, such as warfare or raiding.

Site 54 may have functioned as a marketplace, used by representatives from the intermontane basin and from those layers of the class-stratified coastal valley society that had access to archaized red-painted pottery vessels.

The house at Site 54 was occupied continuously throughout the year; the house in the village at Old Turquoise and the compound on the tropical village were occupied by a group of individuals with a distinctive physical appearance: The adults had tattooed faces and were missing six front teeth. Its members used distinctive goods, like specular hematite bowls, apparently engaged in long-distance commerce, and were always found in possession of strings of spondylus beads, regardless of whether they resided in the mountains or near mollusk beds where spondylus lived. The strings of spondylus beads may have functioned as money. The group constituted a people-class, whose members engaged in commerce and productive activities, like subsistence or manufacture, that were associated with trafficking in exotic goods along and beyond the frontiers of an expanding state. Both women and men apparently engaged in commerce. The burial at Site 52 suggests that long-distance commerce may have involved adolescent women who herded llamas during Phase A and that it was already associated with the creation of distinctive physical markings—for example, the extraction of six incisors. That is, the people-class appeared about the same time that the residents of the coastal valley began to attack their neighbors and subjugate their own kin and neighbors.

One of the exotic goods they moved was obviously spondylus; another was turquoise from the Old Turquoise region. This blue-green raw material was used exclusively by upper-class women residing or interred at Sites 43 and 44 (Problem 7). The turquoise found in all other contexts in the coastal valley came from local deposits. The contextual information suggests that the ruling class or even the ruling family were the only members of that class-stratified coastal society who had access to the imported turquoise.

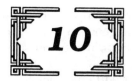

State Formation and the Reorganization of Production and Social Reproduction

STATE FORMATION

State formation is not a unidirectional process. Sometimes states fall apart; sometimes they extend their political hegemony to peoples living elsewhere and incorporate or articulate these political economies with their own. While the extension of power is often understood as conquest, the processes of expansion are rarely indiscriminate ones that merely involve the encapsulation of weaker neighboring communities or polities. Since the extension of power always has underlying motives, the political economy of expansion plays a determinate role in structuring the relations among the metropolitan state, the new subject populations, and the peoples who remain on the margins.

PRODUCTION

While all states are concerned with counting people, collecting taxes, and conscripting workers, distinctive kinds of institutions and practices develop in areas that are incorporated for different reasons and in different ways (Diamond 1951; Thapar 1984). When a state envelops peoples and their lands to extend its own subsistence production, it needs tax assessors, collectors, and overseers to ensure that the subject populations provide the labor, food, and other goods it demands. When a state attempts to control commerce, it must establish control over the groups engaged in production and exchange, over the routes on which the merchants and their goods travel, and over the markets where these items are exchanged. Populations that possess little of interest to the state and its ruling class are frequently encapsulated but not particularly bothered, so long as they acknowledge the sovereignty of the metropolis. In other words, the political-economic and social relations between the metropolitan areas of the state and the subjugated communities are often diverse; each kind of linkage potentially yields a distinctive cultural formation that gives meaning to the uniquely constituted aspects of everyday life in that part of the domain.

SOCIAL REPRODUCTION

Communities encapsulated earlier or located closer to the center of an imperial state are sometimes more dramatically transformed than less assimilated groups toward the periphery. Gradations that exist in time and space reflect different stages in the process of encapsulation, transformation, and acculturation. For instance, during early stages of contact, both imperial garrisons and autonomous border peoples may acquire goods that move along trade routes. As frontier communities become enmeshed in tributary relations, the state may begin to demand the same kinds of goods and/or services received by its traditional authorities. Finally, the traditional social and political-economic structures of the enveloped community may be reorganized to conform to those found in other subject populations. If the encapsulated community acquiesced to tributary relations and political domination, the state may preserve the authority of traditional leaders and incorporate them into the lower echelons of the state apparatus. If the community resisted, the state may replace local persons of authority with its own representatives. As the state rationalizes to reduce cultural diversity or eliminate it altogether, the rights and obligations of the encapsulated community become identical to those imposed elsewhere. With this change, the state could now specify new kinds of tribute—the same ones demanded from subject populations in other areas or from groups incorporated earlier or under similar circumstances.

From the perspective of the communities being encapsulated, the state appears in different forms at various stages in the process. During the initial stage of contact, its presence is confined to isolated garrisons and its contact with the local communities occurs at fixed places; nevertheless, it poses a threat. While the frontier communities retain use rights over their means of production and control over their labor and products, political authority may come to reside more firmly in the hands of privileged members or chieftains, who are able to appropriate increased control over the movement of goods created outside the subsistence sector through activities associated with raiding and trade and through their enhanced ability to create and cement alliances with other peoples. During the later stage when traditional leaders are incorporated into the state apparatus, their autonomy diminishes as their dependence on the state for luxury goods produced by distant peoples and other services increases. The autonomy of the pacified communities is reduced even further as their members begin to participate in institutions and practices and to adopt cultural forms promoted by the state—for example, state cults and pageants, standardized weights and measures, or official languages (Gailey & Patterson 1988).

Archaeologists working in various parts of the world recognize that states have transformed landscapes and reorganized production and social reproduction. They have also recognized that not all states did this in the same way. For instance, between 1438 and 1530, the Inca state in Peru built a series of capital cities and provincial centers throughout their domain. It created strategic hamlets in some regions as dispersed local communities were resettled into larger villages where their members could be supervised and controlled more effectively. It also resettled groups in areas far from their homelands in order to break up the traditional community or to have the colonists spy on their new neighbors. It transformed the diets and consumption patterns of subject communities. It attempted to standardize the production of items, like pottery or textiles, that were employed at various state installations. It appropriated the means of production from subordinated communities; while lands were claimed by both the state apparatus and the ruling class, labor power was extorted to produce goods desired by the state. It also interfered in the demographic and social reproduction of subordinated communities by permanently removing young women from the numbers (Hastorf 1991; Patterson 1991; Silverblatt 1978; Spalding 1984).

By contrast, the Aztecs, who dominated the Triple Alliance of central Mexico during most of the 15th century, built no provincial capitals nor did they attempt to move the capital city itself when a new ruler ascended to the throne. However, the state undertook massive public works that affected the productive and transportation infrastructures of the Valley of Mexico; it consolidated a pan-basin ruling class; it forged new interregional exchange networks and market centers; and it devised new ways for accumulating wealth, labor, and people from subject communities and frontier societies that were ultimately consumed during the state-sponsored ceremonies and that ultimately affected their capacities for demographic and social reproduction (Brumfiel 1983, 1987a, 1987b, 1991; Gledhill 1989).

REFERENCES

Brumfiel, Elizabeth. (1983). Aztec state making: Ecology, structure, and the origin of the state. *American Anthropologist, 85*(2), 261–284.

Brumfiel, Elizabeth. (1987a). Elite and utilitarian crafts in the Aztec state. In Elizabeth M. Brumfiel & Timothy K. Earle (Eds.), *Specialization, exchange and social complexity* (pp. 102–118). Cambridge: Cambridge University Press.

Brumfiel, Elizabeth. (1987b). Consumption and politics at Aztec Huexotla. *American Anthropologist, 89*(4), 679–686.

Brumfiel, Elizabeth. (1991). Weaving and cooking: Women's production in Aztec Mexico. In Joan M. Gero & Margaret W. Conkey (Eds.), *Engendering archaeology: Women and prehistory* (pp. 224–251). Oxford: Basil Blackwell.

Diamond, Stanley. (1951). Dahomey: A Proto-state in West Africa. Ph.D. diss., Columbia University, New York. Ann Arbor, MI: University Microfilms.

Gailey, Christine W., & Thomas C. Patterson. (1988). State formation and uneven development. In Barbara Bender, John Gledhill, & Mogens Larsen (Eds.), *State and society: The emergence and development of social hierarchy and political centralisation* (pp. 77–90). London: George Allen & Unwin.

Gledhill, John. (1989). The imperial form and universal history: Some reflections on relativism and generalization. In Daniel Miller, Michael Rowlands, & Christopher Tilley (Eds.), *Domination and resistance* (pp. 108–126). London: Unwin Hyman.

Hastorf, Christine A. (1991). Gender, space, and food in prehistory. In Joan M. Gero & Margaret W. Conkey (Eds.), *Engendering archaeology: Women and prehistory* (pp. 132–159). Oxford: Basil Blackwell.

Patterson, Thomas C. (1991). *The Inca empire: The formation and disintegration of a pre-capitalist state.* New York & Oxford: Berg.

Silverblatt, Irene. (1978). Andean women in Inca society. *Feminist Studies, 4*(3), 37–61.

Spalding, Karen. (1984). *Huarochiri: An Andean society under Inca and Spanish rule.* Stanford: Stanford University Press.

Thapar, Romila. (1984). The state as empire. In Henri J. M. Claessen & Peter Skalník (Eds.), *The study of the state* (pp. 409–426). Paris: Mouton.

THE DATA AND THE PROBLEM

The following data are from a series of archaeological sites in the intermontane basin described in earlier problems (Figure 10–1). Various lines of evidence indicate that the sites are contemporary with each other and with the coastal valley settlements described in Problem 7. Radiocarbon measurements suggest that these sites, which define Phase C in the basin, also had a duration of 50 to 75 years.

As you will recall, the red-striped pottery of Phase A, which bore resemblances to that of Phase 1, changed dramatically in Phase B, as the basin potters began to manufacture the distinctive blue-painted ware that contrasted with the red-striped and archaized wares produced in the coastal valley during the same period. The shapes and designs of the blue-painted pottery vessels found in the vast majority of the Phase C settlements in the basin are directly derived from Phase B antecedents.

The beginning of Phase C is marked by the complete abandonment and destruction of the palisaded hilltop settlements, the appearance of six villages on arable bottomlands (none of which is located closer than 10 kilometers to one of the hilltop retreats occupied in the preceding phase), the construction of Site 56 (a specialized settlement located equidistant from the contemporary villages), and the village at Site 57.

Site 55   This valley floor village was selected for further excavation and investigation. It closely resembled the other five villages in terms of size, layout, kinds of structures, number of residential units, and presumed population; there was also an adjacent cemetery. The settlement was organized on a grid system. Houses were arranged in blocks that were crosscut by streets intersecting at right angles. There were six blocks of residential structures, each composed of 10 houses associated with one or two outbuildings used for food preparation and storage and occasionally as workshops where fabrics were woven on horizontal looms and pottery or agricultural implements were produced. The residences were rectangular, stone-walled structures with thatched roofs and covered floor areas averaging 51 square meters. Each house opened directly onto a street. Traces of foodstuffs in the refuse and in the clay-lined food storage pits indicate that the inhabitants consumed a variety of cultivated tubers—potatoes, ocas, and ullucos—as well as small quantities of deer and guinea pigs that were kept in shallow corrals next to the kitchen areas. Seasonal indicators show that the settlement was occupied continuously throughout the year. Industrial debris in the midden deposits associated with each house indicates that its members farmed, grew cotton and gourds, wove cotton textiles, hunted a few deer during the winter months, and engaged in limited craft production. The technical division of labor within the domestic units, which seem to have been largely self-sufficient units in terms of the production of subsistence goods, was based largely on gender. Adolescent and adult women spun, wove, cooked, and made pottery, while males farmed and hunted. Some goods—like pottery and wool— circulated within and between the farming villages.

Figure 10–1

A cemetery adjacent to the settlement yielded 200 burials, half of which were infants or juveniles. One-third of the remaining adolescents and adults were females, all of whom exhibited frontal-occipital cranial deformation and effacing of the pubic symphyses, which indicates that they had borne one or more infants. None of the adults survived beyond the age of 35 years. The average statures of the adult males and females were 162 ± 1.3 centimeters and 156 ± 1.4 centimeters, respectively. All of the infants were buried in blue-painted jars. All of the juveniles, adolescents, and adults were interred in flexed position in shallow pits. Each was associated with a Phase C blue-painted plate filled with tubers and with collected or archaized Phase B blue-painted bottles. The adolescent and adult males were also interred with agricultural tools and the females with spinning, sewing, and weaving implements used with backstrap or horizontal looms. Virtually all of the skeletons of adult women showed signs of arthritis in their lower backs, an ailment associated with the kinds of looms they used.

Site 56 This settlement is located on the floor of the basin. It consists of a 100- by 200-meter-square plaza, 500 silos from which maize has been recovered, 50 storehouses that yielded fragments of large textiles woven on vertical looms, two residential structures with covered floor areas of 70 and 140 square meters respectively, a dormitory with a bath and covered floor area of 150 square meters, an adjacent workshop with vertical looms, three kitchens separated from the residential structures, and three types of tombs. Seasonal indicators in the habitation refuse adjacent to the kitchens show that they were used continuously throughout the year; the food prepared in each kitchen area suggests that the residents consumed quantities of maize, maize beer, tubers, guinea pigs, llamas, and deer. Pottery storage and food preparation and serving vessels associated with each of the kitchens were large by local standards: (1) Fragments found in the dormitory kitchen were from red-painted Phase 3 vessels manufactured by the state; (2) fragments found in the kitchen adjacent to the smaller of the two covered residences were also red-painted Phase 3 pieces manufactured in state workshops; and (3) the vessels found in the kitchen associated with the larger residence were locally produced and decorated with local blue-painted stylistic elements or exhibited eclectic combinations of blue-painted and red-painted design elements derived ultimately from the local, state, and several exotic pottery styles.

Domestic refuse associated with the dormitory included large numbers of spindle whorls, broken or discarded weaving implements, and fragments of locally produced blue-painted pottery vessels that imitated the sizes and shapes of Phase 3 vessels manufactured by the state. Domestic refuse associated with the smaller residence contained red-painted pottery manufactured by the state in the coastal valley and counting devices for keeping records. The midden associated with the larger palace contained large quantities of the blue-and-red-painted pottery with eclectic combinations of local, state, and exotic designs and shapes.

There were three distinctive tombs on the margins of Site 56. Tomb 1 was a burial vault that was entered repeatedly. It contained the remains of 93 adult women. The most recent burial was a 25-year-old woman whose body had been placed inside the entrance with three state-produced red-painted pottery vessels; the remainder of the skeletons had been sorted into piles of arms, legs, torsos, and heads that were arranged neatly along the sides of the crypt; all of the skulls exhibited frontal-occipital deformation, like those in the farming villages, and none of the pubic symphyses showed the kind of effacing associated with childbirth. Tomb 2 was also reentered on several occasions. It contained the remains of three adult men, all of whom died in their early forties and were tall by local standards; they were associated with state-produced red-painted plates and jade necklaces. Tomb 3 was also reentered repeatedly; it contained the remains of at least nine individuals who had been cremated; their remains were placed in the elaborate, locally produced jars decorated with eclectic combinations of local, state, and foreign designs; 15 silver plates containing food remains were also placed in the tomb.

Site 57   This settlement is located on the side of an isolated hill in the basin that overlooks the bottomlands. The residents lived in 80 round houses with covered floor areas averaging 40 square meters. Seasonal indicators in the refuse show that it was occupied continuously; the domestic pottery was made with local clays but resembled a style that was used 500 kilometers to the north. The residents also stored their food in pottery vessels made to state specifications by basin potters and in red-painted storage vessels that were produced in the state workshop in the coastal valley. Food remains indicate that they consumed large quantities of deer, llama, tubers, and maize. The members of this enclave practiced a form of cranial deformation that yielded cone-shaped skulls among both males and females. Adolescent and adult men were buried with weapons and agricultural implements; adolescent and adult women were interred with agricultural tools and spinning, sewing, and weaving implements.

Site 58   This set of agricultural terraces, located 1 kilometer from Site 56 near the edge of the valley, was buried and sealed by a mud slide during an exceptionally wet winter. Phase A and B pottery were found in the fill and in the rubble retaining walls; a few Phase C blue-painted potsherds identical to those made and used in Site 55 were scattered on the surface of 28 of the 30 platforms excavated. Soil samples from 30 terraces yielded significant quantities of maize phytoliths (microscopic silica particles derived from plant cells; phytoliths derived from particular genera or species, like maize, have distinctive sizes and shapes that can be viewed with a scanning electron microscope).

Bone collagen was extracted from the skeletal remains of individuals interred in the various cemeteries in order to determine their stable carbon and nitrogen values. These analyses provide a cumulative picture of food consumption. The results indicate (1) that the inhabitants of Site 55 ate mainly tubers, and there was no significant difference between the diet of men and women; (2) that the inhabitants, both males and females, of Site 56 consumed more maize than their contemporaries in the farming villages; the men consumed significantly greater amounts of maize than the women who resided in this settlement; and (3) that the residents of Site 57, both males and females, consumed more maize than the inhabitants of the farming villages but less than the men and women who resided at Site 56; their maize consumption resembled those of the men garrisoned at Site 50 during Phase 2. The men at Site 57 consumed more maize than the women who resided there.

Using information from Problems 7 to 9, construct a chronological chart indicating the relationships between the three phases of social development in the basin and the three developmental phases in the coastal valley.

Given the conditions described in this and earlier problems (especially Problems 7 to 9), what events precipitated the changes described above? That is, what provoked the conditions and patterns of archaeological evidence found in the basin in Phases A to C? What do Sites 55, 56, and 57 as well as the contemporary but unexcavated settlements tell us about the transformations of the landscape and production relations in the basin during Phase C? What do Site 55 and its associated cemetery tell us about the organization of production in the farming villages?

Who lived at Site 56? Who resided in the dormitory? What did they do? Where were they buried? Who lived in the smaller palace? What was their relation to the state? What did they do? Who lived in the larger palace? What was their place in the local class structure?

What is the significance of Site 57? Who lived there? What was their relationship to the state and to the local communities? Were they local people?

What is the significance of the terraces at Site 58? When were they built and used? Who built them? What was grown on them? Who did the agricultural labor? Who consumed the product? Where was it stored or consumed?

What is the significance of the stable carbon and nitrogen isotope values extracted from the bone collagen samples? What do the differences tell us about consumption patterns and the intersection of class, ethnicity, and gender in the basin during Phase C?

DISCUSSION OF THE PROBLEM

Phase C (Problem 10) is entirely contemporary with Phase 3, the most recent unit (Problem 7), in the valley; both have durations of 50 to 75 years. The preceding phases—Phase B in the basin and Phase 2 in the valley—have durations of 80 and 100 years, respectively. This suggests that Phase B is contemporary with all of Phase 2 and with the later part of the period when Phase 1 pottery was produced. Basin Phase A is contemporary with and earlier than Phase 1.

The data suggest that the inhabitants of the intermontane basin had close relations with the residents of the coastal valley during Phase A (and Phase 1). When class formation began to occur in the coastal valley, they severed their ties with the coastal communities, created a distinctive local cultural tradition that included blue-painted pottery and moved to fortified hilltop villages that they defended successfully during Phase B, after the coastal state had established a garrison at Site 50. By the beginning of Phase C, the basin communities were incorporated into the state. The hilltop settlements were destroyed, and their remaining residents were resettled in farming hamlets built on the valley floor at a considerable distance from them. These were open settlements without surrounding walls or palisades. The 60 or so houses in each farming village opened directly onto the street. Households were the basic, seemingly self-sufficient production-consumption units in the villages. Site 56 was an elite center, whose residents were either part of the state apparatus or closely linked with it.

Site 55 was a farming hamlet composed of self-sufficient household production-consumption units with technical divisions of labor based largely on gender: The males farmed and the females processed food, wove on horizontal looms, and possibly engaged in the production of other craft items in the compound. That the women had arthritis, especially in their lower backs, indicates that their work activities were inscribed on their bodies. The style of the pottery they manufactured and used in everyday life and placed in the tombs of the dead derived from or emulated the blue-painted vessels used by their ancestors in the hilltop forts. They also collected Phase B pots and placed them in the tombs of adolescents and adults.

Site 56 was inhabited by young women who were permanently removed from the local community, foreign representatives of the state apparatus, and the local ruling family. The young women, whose crania were deformed in the same way as those residing in the farming villages, lived in the dormitory. They wove wide fabrics on vertical looms and presumably prepared food and beverages for the occupants of the two residential structures, and were buried in Tomb 1. They also do not have children, unlike their sisters in the neighboring farming villages. The state permanently removed both their productive and reproductive capacities from the local village communities and assigned their productive skills to the state and the local ruling family. This placed a heavy burden on the villages, judging by the aberrant sex ratios found in the cemetery at Site 55.

The smaller residential structure at Site 56 was inhabited by a representative of the state who—judging by the counting devices found in the refuse and tombs—kept records and presumably acted as an overseer. The jade necklaces found in Tomb 2 suggest this office was filled by members of the warrior stratum from the coastal valley. The larger residence at Site 56 was inhabited by the local ruling family who were distinguished from the local population by burial practices and by the eclectic red-and-blue-painted pottery they used in the course of everyday life.

Site 57 was inhabited by a culturally distinct group—presumably a state-sponsored and supported enclave from a distant area. Its residents retained their cultural identities after moving into the area. They received food from the state, and presumably the men provided military service on demand. Both men and women farmed, and women produced cloth and garments.

Site 58 consists of terraced agricultural platforms that were built and used during Phase C to grow maize. The construction and the agricultural labor was probably provided by men who resided in Site 55 or one of the other farming villages. The crop was grown for the state, stored in the silos at Site 56, and used mainly by the residents of Site 56 and, to a much smaller extent, by the residents of Site 57. It suggests that the state appropriated labor power rather than particular goods from the male subjects of the basin.

The stable carbon and nitrogen isotope values provide some indication of what the various populations consumed during their lifetimes. The men and women who lived in the farming villages ate the same foods in similar quantities. The men and women who resided at Site 56 consumed significantly more maize during their lifetimes than their contemporaries in the farming villages; the males at Site 56 consumed more maize than the females who resided there. The men and women at Site 57 consumed more maize than their neighbors in the farming villages and less than the men or women at Site 56; again, the males consumed more maize than the females.

The consumption patterns reflect the class structure of the region:

(1) direct producers residing in farming villages with no significant differences in the consumption patterns of men and women; (2) a small group of elite men and women who resided at Site 56; the men consumed more maize than the women at the site and their contemporaries elsewhere in the basin; and (3) the men and women of the retainer population at Site 57, who originated outside the basin, consumed maize from the state stores; the males consumed more than the women. There were also gender differences in the consumption patterns of the state-related dominant class and retainer population.

The Social Construction of Gender, Ethnicity, and Race

Gender, ethnicity, and race are socially constructed categories that organize the production and reproduction of everyday life. An individual's identity and place in a society are not based on the presence or absence of some essentialist feature in his or her physical appearance or biological makeup; they are based instead on the complex interplay of various historically constituted institutions, conditions, and practices. Socially constructed and reproduced heritages, degree of integration into a particular polity, class position, or participation in groups and activities proclaims or reaffirms membership and delineates the nature of the affiliation. The form, significance, and even existence of these categories have varied and continue to vary in important ways from one society to another and within one society through time; on a global scale, race, for example, does not seem to have been a particularly important social category before the advent of the Atlantic slave trade and the formation of settler colonies (Drinnon 1980).

GENDER

Gender differences refer to the ways in which sexual differences that are perceived to be natural are constructed. There are two levels of construction. The first level is concerned with what a particular concrete society considers natural; biology, occupation, preference, age, and possession of female essence are only a few of the criteria that various societies, mentioned in the ethnographic and historical literature, have used to circumscribe and give substance to the meaning of natural. The second level attaches significance to the sexual differences that have been selected to constitute men, women, or other genders (Gailey 1988). For instance, the Hua of highland New Guinea simultaneously separate the sexes and reclassify the gendered identities of individuals during their lifetimes. This is related to the expulsion or acquisition of female essence. All children possess this essence from birth and by virtue of continued proximity to their mothers. Boys lose the essence when they move into the men's house and are initiated into the secrets of manhood; however, they gradually regain it through the consumption of foods necessary for growth and maturation and through sexual intercourse. Females lose the essence through menstruation and childbirth. Postmenopausal women who have given birth at least three times have lost all female essence; they move into the men's house and are initiated into the secrets of male society. Older men have acquired so much female essence through food consumption and intercourse that they are classified with children and women who have had fewer than three infants. They move out of the men's house and assume the forms of labor, authority, dress, sitting, and residence that are appropriate to their new gender identity (Meigs 1976).

ETHNICITY

An ethnic community or group—what is called an *ethnie* in French and an *etnia* in Spanish—have a number of distinctive features that underpin and delineate the boundaries, sense of belonging, and sentiments of those individuals who claim membership. These include (1) a common or collective name known and used by members who identify and distinguish themselves from others; (2) myths of origins and descent that provide not only a place of origin but also a location in the world and a framework of meaning that makes sense of the community's experiences, defines its essence, inspires collective action, and allows its members to define themselves in relation to others; (3) a sense of shared history that unites successive generations, each with their own particular experiences; (4) a shared culture—for example, customs, language, art, music, or symbols—that uniquely marks identity and shapes boundaries; (5) an association with a symbolic geographical center, a homeland, in which the members reside or to which they return; and (6) a sense of community and solidarity (Smith 1986; Wobst 1977). As Comaroff (1987) points out, ethnicity and ethnic groups are always the products of particular historical circumstances and have their origins in specific historical and social forces. This means that they are neither a "primordial feature of human organization" nor an explanatory "first cause" in spite of their reality or the actions that are regularly carried out to defend their name and honor.

RACE

The ideology of race claims that races as biologically rather than socially constituted categories actually exist and that individuals possess inherited biological characteristics that somehow define or determine their identity and membership in one or another group (Stark, Reynolds, & Lieberman 1979). The ideology of racism alleges that there is a natural hierarchy of races and that this legitimates power relations and the subordination of one race by another (Kovel 1984). However, race is also a socially constructed category. For example, quasi-racial categories—like Spaniard, Indian, and mestizo—were created as the relationship between colonizer and colonized crystallized in the New World; they were constituted and sustained by state institutions and practices as integral parts of the conquest of the Iberian Peninsula and the New World. While state officials were particularly exercised about the status and fiscal obligations of mestizos—the offspring of unions between colonizer and colonized—these statuses were not fixed. One avenue of social mobility was provided by moving and acculturation; another involved purchasing a certificate from the church that confirmed that the buyers were the "pure-blooded" descendants of old Spanish Christian families and that none of their ancestors were Jews, Moors, or heretics. At the same time that wealthy *Indios*, *Negros*, and *Mestizos* were purchasing these certificates, some Spaniards were forging documents to pass themselves off as members of the Indian nobility in order to lay claim to the wealth, lands, and right of succession to office possessed by certain native families (Patterson 1991).

Class and state formation and the trajectories of uneven development they promote create conditions for the transformation of gender relations. As Gailey (1992) notes, the gender equality of kin-organized communities is distorted and ultimately replaced by various kinds of gender hierarchies: (1) Gender parallelism emerges in societies, like the Inca empire, where men and women in the same strata retain significant amounts of authority but the state creates an overarching symbolic structure that associates rulership with masculinity; (2) patriarchy appears in states, like Classical Athens, that make the conjugal family household central to social reproduction and that vest power in the social and symbolic roles of the father and husband; and (3) masculinism, which appears in those societies, like the United States, that associates power with attributes and behaviors that are considered masculine.

Class and state formation also underwrite the conditions for the constitution of ethnic communities, racial groups, and racist ideologies. States are genocidal and ethnocidal; they destroy people and obliterate or marginalize local cultural traditions and practices. They prevent local kin communities from re-creating autonomous ways of life and limit their capacity for self-determination. In the context of state formation, peoples that attempt to retain control over their resources, products, and labor—the conditions necessary for them to retain a way of life—are frequently threatened with annihilation, dispersal, enslavement, or some other form of state-sponsored repression. However, these kin communities may forge new identities in opposition to the state-sponsored ideologies of unity and citizenship; this may involve a particular group, or it may involve individuals from a number of groups, whose basis for identity is recognition of their shared position and commonality of interests in a state-sponsored division of labor (Gailey & Patterson 1987). Frequently, these new identities include the creation of authentic practices or symbols at the same time they incorporate and translate features forged by the state.

REFERENCES

Comaroff, John L. (1987). Of totemism and ethnicity: Consciousness, practice and the signs of inequality. *Ethnos, 52*(3), 301–323.

Drinnon, Richard. (1980). *Facing West: The metaphysics of Indian-hating and empire-building.* New York: New American Library.

Gailey, Christine W. (1988). Evolutionary perspectives on gender hierarchy. In Beth B. Hess & Myra M. Ferree (Eds.), *Analyzing gender: A handbook of social science research* (pp. 32–67). Newbury Park, CA: Sage.

Gailey, Christine W. (1992, July 6-7). *The uneven development of patriarchy: State formation, economic development, and trajectories of gender hierarchy.* Paper presented at World Institute for Development Economics Research, Helsinki.

Gailey, Christine W., & Thomas C. Patterson. (1987). Power relations and state formation. In Thomas C. Patterson & Christine W. Gailey (Eds.), *Power relations and state formation* (pp. 1–26). Washington, DC: American Anthropological Association.

Kovel, Joel. (1984). *White racism: A psychohistory.* New York: Columbia University Press.

Meigs, Anna S. (1976). Male pregnancy and the reduction of sexual opposition in a New Guinea highlands society. *Ethnology*, *15*(4), 393–407.

Patterson, Thomas C. (1991). *Race and archaeology: A comparative and historical view*. Paper presented at the annual meeting of the American Anthropological Association, Chicago.

Smith, Anthony D. (1986). *The ethnic origins of nations*. Oxford & New York: Basil Blackwell.

Stark, Jerry A., Larry T. Reynolds, & Leonard Lieberman. (1979). The social basis of conceptual diversity: A case study of the concept of "race" in physical anthropology. *Sociology of Knowledge, Sciences and Art*, *2*, 87-99.

Wobst, H. Martin. (1977). Stylistic behavior and information exchange. In *For the director: Research essays in honor of James B. Griffin. Museum of Anthropology, University of Michigan, Ann Arbor, Anthropology Papers*, no. 61, pp. 317–342.

THE DATA AND THE PROBLEM

The following data are from archaeological sites located in the intermontane basin discussed earlier (see Figure 11-1). Further studies were also made of the excavated data described in Problems 9 and 10.

Analyses of the habitation refuse associated with each house compound at Site 55—the Phase C farming village—revealed the existence of large numbers of human figurine fragments; those whose sex could be identified were exclusively female. The individuals depicted in the figurines wore breastplates and wide belts and held straight-sided beakers in their hands. Reanalyses of the refuse associated with domestic structures at Sites 51 and 53—the Phase A and B settlements in the intermontane—revealed the complete absence of figurine fragments in both sites.

Site 55 (Problem 10)   A small-scale excavation conducted in a house destroyed by fire revealed two female figurines placed in the northwest corner of the structure; two Phase C blue-painted plates and one Phase B plate filled with fragments of burned cloth had been placed in front of the figurines.

Site 53 (Problem 9)   A small excavation in the extreme northwest corner of this Phase B fortified hilltop settlement uncovered a cache of objects buried under the floor of a destroyed structure. The cache consisted of a life-sized copper breastplate, a wide leather belt with a copper buckle, a straight-sided wooden beaker, and several elaborate embroidered and tapestry fabrics produced on backstrap looms. The cache was found underneath four Phase C female figurines that had

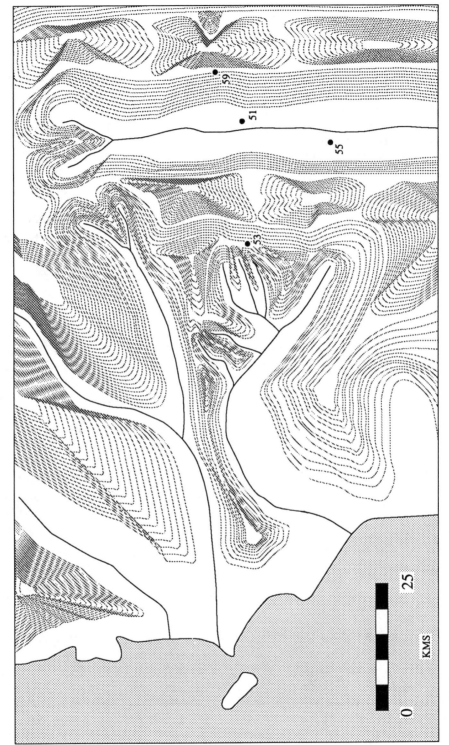

Figure 11–1

been carefully covered with cloth and debris from the burned building.

Site 59   Excavations at this hilltop site revealed rectangular plaza, measuring 10 by 15 meters, that was outlined with boulders. A 3-meter-tall natural slab of rock had been carried to the site and embedded in a 50-centimeter-deep hole. Thin layers of refuse had accumulated around the base of the slab. The earliest layer contained fragments of Phase A pottery, llama bones, scraps of cloth, and cultivated tubers. The second layer contained Phase B potsherds, cloth scraps, and cultivated tubers. The third layer contained Phase C potsherds and food remains but no cloth fragments.

Using the data presented in Problems 9 and 10 and the inferences you have drawn from them, discuss how gender relations and ethnicity developed in the intermontane basin. When and under what conditions do class structures appear? How were gender relations transformed in circumstances shaped by class and state formation?

What inferences can be drawn from the reanalyses of the data from Sites 51, 53, and 55? Who made the cloth offerings?

What is Site 59? What changes occurred there? Who produced the offerings? Do they suggest or reflect changes in gender relations? How are these related to the data revealed in the excavations at Site 59? What inferences can be drawn regarding the transformation of gender relations and their linkages with constructed heritages? Do the data from Sites 53 and 59 suggest men and women each control the objects of their labor power?

When and under what conditions does ethnicity appear? How do gender, ethnicity, and class intersect in the intermontane basin during Phase C?

How are the gender, ethnic, and class structures of the intermontane basin linked to those that prevailed at the same time during Phase 3 in the coastal valley at the same time (Problem 7)?

DISCUSSION OF THE PROBLEM

The data of Problem 9 indicate that the society of the intermontane basin was kin-organized during Phases A and B. There was no social division of labor; however, technical divisions of labor based on age and gender—for example, adult men and women farmed, and teenagers herded—organized various production activities. While households were the basic units of appropriation, the production activities of males and females who resided in them were autonomous and complementary. The items they produced were shared with each other; a few goods—for example, pottery or wool—also found their way to other homesteads. The technical division of labor was modified in Phase B, when the residents of the basin built and moved into fortified hilltop villages; however, there is no evidence for a social division of labor or for the appearance of social inequalities based on gender. Women wove, men farmed, and both defended their settlements from marauders.

The data presented in Problem 10 indicate that a transformation occurred in Phase C, as classes formed in the society and it was incorporated into the coastal state. Physically, the women of the basin were marked by cranial deformation; they prepared food, wove, and engaged in craft production—activities that could have been carried out within the confines of the individual homestead. The state also removed young women from their natal villages, forever depriving their kin and neighbors of their productive and reproductive capacities. The combination of production centered largely at the household level and resistance to the appropriation of young women by the state could create circumstances where older men and women might attempt to hide the identities and even the existence of younger women from state officials and to retain control over their movements. Such actions would lay the foundations for increasing patriarchal relations within the household and the class of direct producers residing in the farming communities. The young women seized by the state, who lived and died at Site 56, were treated very differently in life and death from their sisters in the villages; they were viewed and used by the state as producers of textiles. Since the local ruling class was cremated, the remains found in Tomb 3 tell us very little about how the activities of everyday life of that class were shaped by gender considerations; there is no reason to assume, however, that they were identical to those of the direct producers in the villages.

The reanalyses of the domestic refuse suggest that ritual practices involving the use of female figurines in the corners of peasant households appeared suddenly during Phase C, when the intermontane communities were incorporated into the state. The cloth offerings were probably produced by women residing in the houses. The excavation at Site 53, the hilltop fort, indicate that related activities were also carried out surreptitiously at this abandoned Phase B hilltop fort. The practices involved one or more women who wore copper breastplates and wide belts, the use of wooden beakers, and offerings of time-consuming embroideries and tapestries made by women in the farming villages. The practices also involved collecting and using Phase B pottery vessels.

Site 59 was the locus of ritual practices that began in Phase A and continued through Phase C. These involved offerings of items produced by both men and women during Phases A and B. In Phase C, the offerings, with the possible exception of the pottery, are associated exclusively with the agricultural pursuits of men who reside in the farming villages.

The data suggest that men and women participated in the same ritual practices during Phases A and B and that their ritual practices became spatially differentiated during Phase C. The men's practices continued to occur at public places, known historically, while the women from the farming villages began to conduct their practices in their homes or secretly at an abandoned hilltop fort. At a symbolic level, the males traced their ancestry to the kin-organized community that existed in Phase A, whereas the women focused their activities on the present and linked their plight and present circumstances with the events that occurred during Phases B and C—the hilltop forts and subordination by the state. State formation created a private (secret) domain that became the sphere of women's activities in Phase C, whereas the men from the peasant communities took over the more visible aspects of ritual offerings at historically known shrines, like the one uncovered at Site 59.

The ritual offerings made at Sites 53 and 59 during Phase C suggest that both men and women exerted control over the objects they produced, even though these were shared within the confines of the household.

Ethnicity was also a product of class and state formation. Highly visible markers, which appeared at various times during Phases B and C, increasingly differentiated the population of the intermontane basin from their contemporaries in the coastal valley and from the merchant people-class—the tattooed people with no apparent finite territory—who moved along and beyond the state frontiers in Phase B. The earliest in the intermontane basin involved the production of the distinctive blue-painted pottery of Phase B, which marked a break with the indigenous tradition and with the pottery used in the coastal valley during Phase 2. This tradition was intensified in Phase C as the direct producers collected and imitated locally produced, blue-painted pottery vessels and placed them in tombs. The physical marking was also intensified during Phase C, as female infants in the basin had their skulls deformed; this differentiated them physically from contemporary women in the coastal valley—both the direct producers and those who lived off the labor of others. It also differentiated the local community from the colonists who resided at Site 58 and were sustained partly by the state.

The ruling family/class in the intermontane attempted to legitimate its position by virtue of its relation to the conquest state and to foreigners. The material goods buried in Tomb 3 at Site 56 included silver plates, which were used exclusively by the ruling class in the coastal valley, and the pottery burial urns that were decorated with eclectic combinations of local, state, and foreign designs. The burial practices as well as the grave goods placed in the ruling class tombs at

Site 44 were quite different from those of the provincial rulers who resided at Site 56 (Problem 7). The only feature they had in common were vessels or containers made from silver. Unlike their contemporaries in the basin, the members of the ruling class of the coastal valley attempted to root their position in terms of history; that is, they looted tombs and made extensive use of archaized pottery vessels that combined elements of earlier pottery styles found in the region.

The class structure in the coastal valley was more textured than that found in the intermontane basin. The data presented in Problem 7 indicate that the state apparatus appropriated labor at the village level in the coastal valley—that is, men and women came to Site 37 each year to make goods for the state and were supported by foodstuffs produced and appropriated from the local farming communities. There was also a local male warrior stratum, whose members resided at Site 38, wore jade pendants, and had better diets than the direct producers; they may have been cadet lines in the ruling class, whose members did not or could not ascend to the throne. They served as provincial overseers, judging by jade necklaces found in Tomb 2 at Site 56. Their wives probably came from local farming communities in the coastal valley and enjoyed better diets during their adult years than women engaged in direct production. There was also a group of men and women who worked as full-time craft specialists, who were attached to the state, and whose status was marked by turquoise necklaces; there were no indications of gender inequalities among this group of workers. The ruling class woman interred in the carved coffin in the more recent tomb at Site 44 was the only female associated with jade; this may indicate the emergence of gender parallelism, in which the ruling class becomes symbolically linked with masculine, military activities and subject communities and subordinated peoples are symbolically viewed as female by the state and its rulers.

Class Struggle
and Resistance

CLASS STRUCTURES AND EXPLOITATION

State formation is a regional process that produces a mosaic of different kinds of societies. The class structures that emerge are the collective expression of exploitation—that is, the appropriation of the labor power and products of one group by the members of another (de Ste. Croix 1984: 106-107). Because of exploitation, class conflict is the fundamental relationship between classes. This promotes kin-civil conflicts at home, when the state resolves the contradictions and ambiguities of everyday life in ways that favor one group over another. It creates new tensions in frontier areas, both when the states attempt to encapsulate frontier peoples and when these communities resist subordination, annexation, or conquest. If exploitation is the most distinctive feature of any class-based society, then resistance, its mirror image, must be equally symptomatic. As a result, state-based societies are inherently unstable.

CLASS STRUGGLES

Although the settings in which the members of subject classes conduct their lives are only partly of their own creation, this does not mean that they are completely without power or some degree of control over their lives. As Scott (1985) has pointed out, various forms of passive resistance by subject populations, which avoid either defiance of authority or direct confrontation with it, have been common throughout human history. They probably have been more typical than either open rebellion or revolution. At different times and places, these weapons of the weak have included acts of foot-dragging, misrepresentation, deception, noncompliance, evasion, desertion, pilfering, sabotage, and arson. The constant, more circumspect forms of class struggle rely on implicit understandings and informal networks and require little coordination or planning. Weapons such as these have limited or thwarted the aspirations of many dominant classes. They have been used to mitigate or deny the claims made by the dominant classes or to advance claims against them.

RESISTANCE

Resistance is always more than a collection of individual acts. People give meaning to their acts through thought and symbols. The artistic and ideological forms they create constitute the background to their activities. Scott (1985: 336) has suggested that the weak attempt to penetrate, neutralize, and negate the hegemony of the dominant classes and the state by using the values and rationale of the earlier social order to press their claims and disparage their opponents. However, the subject classes have no monopoly on these techniques, for both states and emerging dominant classes also rework and give new meanings to established institutions and practices to justify new forms of extortion by promoting an illusion of continuity. This is why tradition and the past are always contested terrains that are never surrendered without a struggle.

Archaeological evidence from the Ica Valley of southern Peru provides insight into a situation where the local lords supported the Incas while the peasants clung tenaciously to their own artistic traditions. Only the higher levels of the local nobility used Inca pottery vessels or pottery made locally to Inca specifications; this was also true for pottery that combined features of the local and Inca styles. These three types of pottery were used exclusively at the elite residential center both before and after the valley was incorporated into the imperial state. The peasant villagers used pottery vessels, decorated with traditional local designs, rather than ones that imitated the Inca style. They also looted tombs for antique pottery vessels of types that were manufactured and used in the valley when it was free of Inca domination. After the collapse of Inca political control, the peasants reasserted the dominance of the local artistic tradition, purging it of all traces of Inca influence. It was an artistic revival of the old styles—the ones preferred by the peasantry rather than those adopted by the nobles during the period of foreign domination (Patterson 1986).

The growth of a state apparatus concerned primarily with taxation and policing speaks of a certain reluctance or lack of enthusiasm on the part of its subjects to satisfy the demands of the rulers. However, their resistance to the state was not always passive. Sometimes it erupted into open rebellion. Such revolts often began when subject peoples assassinated the state officials placed among them to spy and collect taxes. Their murders were precipitated by various circumstances—rumors of an emperor's death, opposition to being ruled, or the hope of casting off the demands of the state. These insurrections were often regional. Archaeologists and historians have devoted a considerable amount of attention to the decline of civilization and the collapse of states (Tainter 1988; Yoffee & Cowgill 1988).

For example, parts of the capital city of Teotihuacán were destroyed by fire about the same time that its structure was being transformed (Millon 1988: 149-156). Most of the violent destruction and burning were confined to state buildings—the palaces, public buildings, temples, and pyramids on the Street of the Dead and the state shrines and associated buildings in other parts of the city. At least 147 structures located on the Street of the Dead and nearly half of the temples located elsewhere were burned. By contrast, only about 10 percent of the apartment compounds show evidence of burning during the Metepec Phase. The destruction that did occur was extensive and apparently occurred during a very brief period of time. All of the structures in the Ciudadela were burned; across the street, all but three apartment groups in the Great Compound were destroyed. Stones were removed from the Plaza of the Moon and scattered; walls were toppled in the Puma Mural Group, the Ciudadela palaces, and the Temple of Quetzalcoatl. Richly adorned individuals living in the North Palace of Ciudadela were murdered and dismembered, and there was extensive looting of both the apartment and its rich tombs before the building was destroyed. These buildings were never rebuilt. Fifty years after their destruction, a much smaller population, whose members had either remained in the city or returned after the devastation, continued to live in the apartment compounds located away from the old center; however, they no longer dominated everyday life in central Mexico as their predecessors had done.

The individuals who burned the civic center and public buildings of Teotihuacán and murdered its rulers were *teotihuacanos*, since no foreign persons or artifacts have been found. While they may have had a few allies from the outside, the lower classes responded violently to the increased burdens that the ruling class and the state were attempting to impose. It was the direct producers of Teotihuacán society who destroyed the state and the city, who brought about new settlement patterns and a redistribution of wealth, and who eliminated the exploitative relationship that had existed for centuries between the inhabitants of the city and the surrounding countryside. The destruction of Teotihuacán was apparently a manifestation of a wider rebellion that occurred in Mesoamerica during the eighth and ninth centuries, judging by the destruction of public buildings, the defacing and scattering of monuments extolling the deeds of rulers, and the abandonment of civic centers in the Maya lowlands (Hamblin & Pitcher 1980; Patterson 1993).

REFERENCES

de Ste. Croix, Geoffrey E. M. (1984). Class in Marx's conception of history, ancient and modern. *New Left Review*, no. 146, 94–111.

Hamblin, R. L., & B. L. Pitcher. (1980). The classic Maya collapse: Testing class conflict hypotheses. *American Antiquity*, 45, 246–267.

Millon, René. (1988). The last years of Teotihuacán dominance. In Norman Yoffee & George L. Cowgill (Eds.), *The collapse of ancient states and civilizations* (pp. 102–164). Tucson: University of Arizona Press.

Patterson, Thomas C. (1986). Ideology, class formation, and resistance in the Inca state. *Critique of Anthropology*, 6(1), 75–85.

Patterson, Thomas C. (1993). Las sociedades nucleares de Mesoamerica. *Historia General de América.*

Scott, James C. (1985). *Weapons of the weak: Everyday forms of peasant resistance.* New Haven & London: Yale University Press.

Tainter, Joseph A. (1988). *The collapse of complex societies.* Cambridge: Cambridge University Press.

Yoffee, Norman, & George L. Cowgill (Eds.). (1988). *The collapse of ancient states and civilizations.* Tucson: University of Arizona Press.

THE DATA AND THE PROBLEM

The data presented here are from a series of contemporary archaeological sites in the regions discussed in Problems 7 through 11 (shown in Figure 12-1). Analysis of chronologically sensitive pottery forms and designs, associations indicating contemporaneity, and an extensive series of absolute dates from various materials associated with the events and sites mentioned below indicate that they date to a period spanning about 50 years.

The Intermontane Basin

The design elements and forms of the distinctive blue-painted Phase D pottery produced in the intermontane basin were derived exclusively from the kinds of pottery used in the farming villages and in the abandoned Phase B settlements. All traces of state and foreign influence and the kinds of decoration associated with the local elite during the preceding phase had been purged by local potters. In addition, some potters began to make red-painted vessels from local clays. The antecedents of these vessels are found in the Phase 3 styles of the peasant villages in the coastal valley.

Site 55 (Problems 10 and 11) This settlement and the other five farming villages in the basin were largely abandoned toward the end of Phase C and during the early part of Phase D; however, three of the houses in one block continued to be occupied by individuals who farmed and used both the distinctive blue-painted Phase D of the basin and the red-painted pottery vessels, made from local clays, that resembled the Phase 4 vessels produced in the coastal valley. Two houses in the village were occupied by individuals who initially used only red-painted Phase 4 vessels made from coastal valley clays and subsequently used locally made Phase 4 and Phase D pottery— that is, the intrusive coastal style and the locally derived blue-painted style.

Site 56 (Problems 10 and 11) At the end of Phase C, the dormitory and adjacent workshop and the two residential structures were destroyed by fire. The occupants of the two palaces, but not the dormitory, were dismembered and their remains scattered before the buildings were set on fire. The maize, tapestries made on vertical looms, and other objects and foodstuffs placed in the 500 silos and 50 storehouses were gradually removed during Phase D.

Site 57 (Problem 11) This hillside settlement was abandoned early in Phase D, and many of the round domestic structures were burned at the time. After a short interval, four rectangular houses with covered floor spaces averaging 50 square meters were built. Seasonal indicators show that the hamlet was occupied continuously throughout the year; domestic remains indicate that the residents

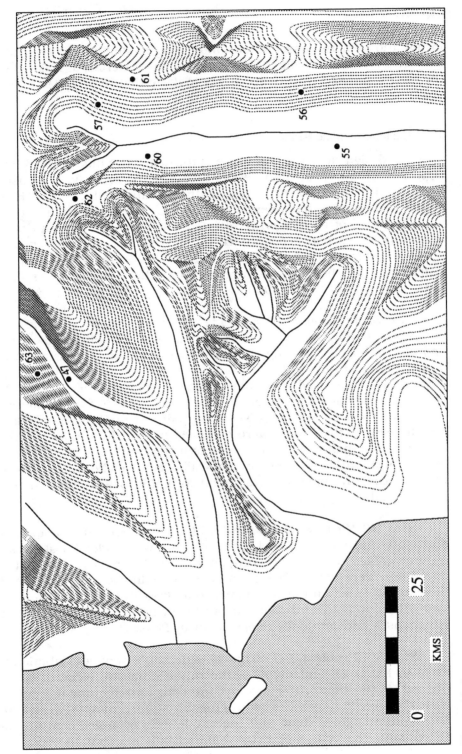

Figure 12–1

farmed, herded llamas, wove, made agricultural implements, and produced pottery that resembled the contemporary red-painted pottery made and used in the Phase 4 settlements in the coastal valley.

Site 60   This is 1 of 12 farming hamlets that were built and occupied during Phase D, all located in close proximity to the small, dispersed villages that were abandoned toward the end of Phase A. It was selected as representative of this kind of settlement. It is located on the bottomlands of the basin near a spring. The excavations revealed the remains of eight rectangular, wattle-and-daub houses with covered floor areas of about 49 square meters. Seasonal indicators in the habitation refuse show that the hamlet was occupied continuously throughout the year; however, the most intensive occupation occurred from the spring to early fall. Domestic debris shows that all of the domestic groups farmed, raised guinea pigs and llamas, spun and wove both cotton and woolen cloth on backstrap looms, and kept a few llamas in pens at the rear of the house compounds. The refuse associated with each house also revealed numbers of blue-painted Phase D figurine fragments.

Excavations in a burned house revealed the existence of small shrines in the northwest corner. It consisted of two female figurines and a plate filled with charred bits of cloth manufactured on a backstrap loom.

Fifty infants and children placed in blue-painted jars and 40 adolescent and adult individuals were interred in flexed positions were uncovered in a cemetery adjacent to the settlement. Genetic studies of the skeletal remains indicated that most of the males, the adolescent females, and some of the adult females were closely related. Analyses of the stable carbon and nitrogen values of the 40 adolescent and adult individuals indicate that males and females had similar diets, that both consumed tubers, maize, and meat, and that they ate more maize and meat than the peasants who lived in the Phase C farming settlements. Most of the females exhibiting cranial deformation came from the stratigraphically earlier burials in the cemetery; the females interred in the cemetery later in the end of the phase showed no evidence of frontal-occipital cranial deformation. Many of the females also showed signs of arthritis in their lower backs. Adolescent and adult males were interred with weapons, agricultural implements, and blue-painted Phase D plates filled with peanuts and chili peppers; the grave goods associated with adolescent and females included spindles, sewing and weaving implements, weapons, pottery making tools, and blue-painted Phase D plates filled with peanuts and chili peppers. Many of the earlier burials were interred with tapestries woven on vertical looms. Many of the men and women interred in the later part of Phase D were buried with small tapestry fabrics and spondylus beads.

Site 61   This was one of seven Phase D camps found in the high grasslands around the intermontane basin. It consisted of two rectangular, semisubterranean, stone-walled houses with floor areas of 25 square meters and a circular enclosure filled with llama dung. Seasonal indicators in the refuse next to the houses show that they were occupied intermittently and mainly from late fall and early spring. The residents consumed fetal and neonatal llamas in January and February.

Site 62   This small settlement was located about 6 kilometers from the old garrison at Site 50 and 3 kilometers from Site 54 (Problem 9). It consisted of one stone-walled house with a covered floor area of 60 square meters. It was occupied continuously throughout the year by individuals who left caches of spondylus shell and of tapestry fabrics made on vertical looms underneath the clay floor. Its residents tilled a field next to the house, kept llamas in a nearby corral, and made circular spondylus beads. Judging by the domestic refuse found next to the house, the inhabitants used locally made Phase D blue-painted pottery and red-painted Phase 4 pottery as well as specular hematite vessels that were not made from local clays.

The Coastal Valley

Widespread changes also occurred during this period in the nearby state-based society of the coastal valley described in Problem 7. The large farming settlements at Sites 31, 33, and 35 were completely abandoned at the beginning of Phase 4 (which is completely contemporary with Phase D in the intermontane basin). The textile and weapons-producing workshops that were staffed seasonally by residents from the farming villages quickly fell into disuse, and the food storage facilities were emptied. The craft specialists who resided in the workshop-residential structures at Site 40 and produced jewelry and other goods for the state and the ruling class dispersed. Offerings were no longer made at the pyramid at Site 41; however, the pyramid itself was not damaged. The inhabitants of 18 of the warriors' houses at Site 38 were murdered and their houses burned toward the end of Phase 3. The inhabitants of the house associated with the pyramid at Site 41 and the palatial residence at

Site 43 were murdered and dismembered before the structures were burned toward the end of Phase 3. Radiocarbon samples from materials associated with the burned structures suggest that the fires occurred at the same time.

Site 47 (Problem 8) This was 1 of the 18 hilltop forts built during Phase 1 and was reoccupied briefly near the beginning of Phase 4 by about 50 individuals. Seasonal indicators in the Phase D refuse indicate that the occupation was continuous and may have lasted only a few years. Domestic refuse indicates that the inhabitants manufactured slings, stone-headed maces, and spear-thrower darts.

Two adult males were buried during Phase 4 next to one of the houses that was reoccupied. Both had received severe depressed skull fractures and were interred with jade necklaces.

Site 63 This is 1 of 19 households or hamlets that were built during Phase 4 in steep, relatively inaccessible side canyons. It was representative of the small settlements found in these refuge areas. It consisted of a single house compound with three residential structures. The inhabitants lived there from late spring to fall with a small llama herd. They cultivated maize and other plants in a small garden, collected seasonally wild plants and nuts, hunted deer, and trapped birds. They made red-painted Phase 4 pottery, agricultural implements, and stone dart points that were used with spearthrowers. They wore clothing woven from llama wool.

What happened at Site 56 toward the end of Phase C and the during Phase D? How does the evidence of looting relate to the evidence provided by the skeletons and grave goods in the hamlet at Site 60? What light does the evidence from Site 55 shed on the events that occurred in the farming villages? Who resided at Site 55? Where did they come from? What happened at Site 57? Who were the new residents? What does this suggest about the events that were taking place in the coastal valley? What kind of landscape was beginning to take shape in the basin in Phase D?

What happened at Site 60? What do the nitrogen and carbon values indicate? Who controlled distribution of goods they produced? What does the cemetery population indicate about cranial deformation? Which individuals were most closely related in the settlement, and what does this indicate about patterns of matrimonial mobility? Who controlled distribution of goods they produced? What does the cemetery population indicate about cranial deformation? Which individuals were most closely related in the settlement, and what does this indicate about patterns of matrimonial mobility? What heritage was constructed by the peasant villagers? What events or episodes of the past were extolled? Who created material representations of this heritage? What does Site 61 represent? What goods were exchanged?

Describe the events that occurred in the coastal valley at the end of Phase 3 and during Phase 4. How was the landscape transformed? Using the grave goods as indicators, which class reused Site 47? Who built and occupied the households and hamlets in the refuge areas? What forces of class formation and disintegration may have occurred in the coastal valley during Phase 4?

DISCUSSION OF THE PROBLEM

The residential structures and workshop at Site 56 were destroyed toward the end of Phase C, at the same time or shortly after the local elite and state officials residing in them were slain and dismembered. Judging by the fact that none of the local women in the dormitory were apparently harmed, it is reasonable to infer that their kin and neighbors were involved in the murders that led to the dismantling of the state apparatus in the intermontane basin. The fact that tapestries made on vertical looms eventually appear as grave goods and that peasant diets at Site 60 had improved suggests that the local residents also looted the grain silos and storehouses during Phase D.

For the most part, the residents of the peasants abandoned the rigidly planned, strategic hamlets imposed by the state in Phase C and returned to dispersed hamlets that were scattered over the bottomlands of the basin. A new regional landscape was crystallizing—one dominated by dispersed farming hamlets, herders' camps in the mountains, the renewed importance of llama herding in the local economy, the absence of state installations, and the reappearance of merchant people on the edge of the basin.

A few local households remained in a farming village at Site 55, where they were joined by and lived next to individuals who had immigrated from the coastal valley. These refugees initially used pottery vessels they brought with them; later they began to use red-painted vessels they made from local clays and blue-painted vessels that were presumably made by their neighbors. There was also a colony of immigrant farmers, herders, and weavers who built rectangular houses among the ruin of Site 57. They also used and made red-painted pottery from the coastal valley or from local clays. The evidence suggests that the population of any basin farming hamlet in Phase D may have been more diverse ethnically than its Phase C predecessors.

Site 60 was one of the new farming settlements. The seasonal indicators show that it was inhabited throughout the year; however, they also suggest that some individuals were going to winter seasonal pastures in the high grasslands around the basin and living in camps like the one excavated at Site 61. Men and women generally had better diets than their immediate ancestors. The genetic studies of the skeletal population suggests that brothers and sisters constituted the core group of the settlement and that there was greater tendency for women to move to the households or hamlets of their husbands. The grave goods also make it clear that men and women owned or possessed the tools they used to make the useful items that circulated within their households and beyond.

The weapons in the burials suggest that both men and women were involved in the insurrection and subsequently remained armed to defend their homes, families, and neighbors. The practice of cranial deformation was apparently linked closely with the state and ceased as soon as the state apparatus was decapitated. The grave goods suggest that both men and women looted the state storehouses and trafficked in goods with the merchant people who resided at Site 62. Boys and men farmed and presumably herded during the winter months. Adolescent and adult women also wove, made pottery, and kept small shrines with female figurines in the northwest corners of their homes; the pottery they manufactured derived entirely from the peasant villages of Phase C and from the vessels that were manufactured when their ancestors lived in the hilltop forts; symbolically, they rooted their heritage in oppression and resistance to the state.

The archaeological record portrays a very different set of events and processes in the coastal valley. The valley bottomlands were completely abandoned by the residents of the farming villages, when the inhabitants of the palaces at Sites 41 and 43 were murdered and the structures were burned. This meant that the textile and weapons workshops at Site 37 also fell into disuse, since there was no one to provide corvee labor to staff them. The craftspeople at Site 40, who were dependent on the state and its ruling class for support, also moved from the area.

The members of many warrior households at Site 38 were murdered, and the inhabitants of the other households fled. The Phase 4 burials at Site 47 indicate that some returned to 1 of 18 Phase 1 hilltop forts that were reoccupied during this period. The lords of these hilltop castles each had a few retainers; however, they had very few subjects to provide labor-service and goods. The peasant tributaries of Phase 3 had dispersed. Some immigrated to the intermontane basin, where they lived side by side with the indigenous inhabitants after the state apparatus and its representatives had been destroyed in that area. Others fled to inaccessible, easily defended refuges in the side canyons, where they lived in dispersed households or small hamlets. Judging by their choices of places to live, they were not willing or easy subjects from whom the warriors could extract tribute. One possible explanation for the rapid disintegration of the state in this region involves (1) the flight of the subject populations to regions where tribute could not be easily extracted and (2) a civil war within the ruling class, perhaps over succession to the throne. Such an explanation would account for the murder and destruction that took place at the palaces and in part of the warrior settlement. The survivors of this dispute fled to the old forts to defend themselves from their ruling-class rivals, enemies, and presumably kinfolk.